"*Living* the Christian faith, in contrast to knowing about it or being enthusiastic in its cause, is a personal, intricate, and quiet art. But not complicated. It is, in fact, incredibly simple, developing as it does from who we are created to be. But the simplicity commonly eludes us in the noisy complications of the world's culture. And so it helps enormously to have a wise and experienced friend to keep things simple and centered for us. Leith Anderson is just such a friend. His companionship will do your soul good."

Eugene H. Peterson
Professor Emeritus of Spiritual Theology
Regent College

"Leith Anderson's *heart for people reaches* with a warmth of embrace through these pages, just as surely as his *head for good sense teaches* with practical insight through them. His many years as a trustworthy pastor, shepherd-of-souls, has distinguished him among his peers. I would encourage anyone to welcome this man to introduce you to new dimensions of friendship with the greatest friend of all."

Jack W. Hayford, Pastor/Chancellor
The Church on the Way
King's College and Seminary

"It is so much easier to be friends with Jesus' friends than friends with Jesus! Leith Anderson helps us redress the balance. The heart is a lonely heart until it finds God. Here is a rich opportunity to understand how that can happen, and more, how having found him, he can fill our lives with a definite purpose and significance."

Jill P. Briscoe
Author, *Prayer That Works*
Minister-at-Large, Elmbrook Church

"Here is a devotional book of delightfully refreshing and unique insights into familiar Scriptures, which will produce that profound new intimate friendship with God so many are seeking today.

"Amazingly, this book propels us along in the narrative, skips effortlessly into fascinating historical trivia, suddenly dives into deep doctrinal truth, and then clinches the point with an inescapable personal application. Absorbed in the excitement of the text, the reader—without even trying—absorbs deep word studies pleasantly sprinkled throughout. Unexpectedly, step by step, the reader emerges with a well-rounded, biblically accurate, precious new intimate relationship with God through Jesus.

"Extremely important to me is the printing of the whole passage of Scripture, letting us see the truth in context for ourselves directly from God. Then, making each one not just abstract theory but personal, which needs to be applied right then, pushes past the intellect into the very heart and life of the reader. And true relational transformation has taken place—with God and the reader.

"Be prepared to be surprised, motivated, questioned, matured, and dramatically changed—enormously enjoying every minute."
Evelyn Christenson
President and Founder, United Prayer Ministry

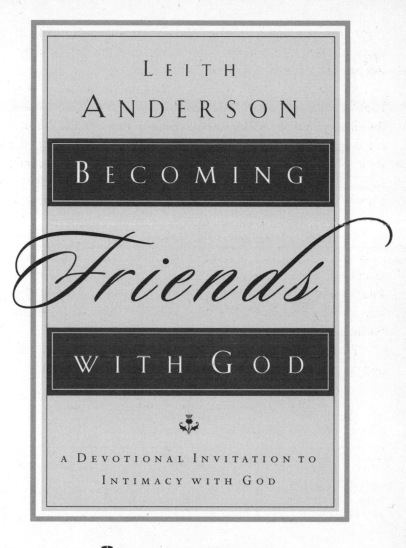

LEITH
ANDERSON

BECOMING

Friends

WITH GOD

A DEVOTIONAL INVITATION TO
INTIMACY WITH GOD

BETHANYHOUSE
Minneapolis, Minnesota

Published by Bethany House Publishers
A Ministry of Bethany Fellowship International
11400 Hampshire Avenue South
Bloomington, Minnesota 55438
www.bethanyhouse.com

Printed in the United States of America by
Bethany Press International, Bloomington, Minnesota 55438

Library of Congress Cataloging-in-Publication Data

Anderson, Leith, 1944-
    Becoming friends with God : a devotional invitation to intimacy with God / by Leith Anderson.
        p. cm.
    ISBN 0-7642-2531-6 (pbk.)
    1. Spirituality. 2. Meditations. I. Title.
    BV4501.3 .A53   2001
    242—dc21   2001002564

LEITH ANDERSON is senior pastor of Wooddale Church in Eden Prairie, Minnesota. Although he is known nationally as an author, speaker, and educator, his first love is the local church and its people. A graduate of Moody Bible Institute, Bradley University, Denver Seminary, and Fuller Theological Seminary, he has written several books including *Leadership That Works* and *Praying to the God You Can Trust*. He and his wife, Charleen, live in Eden Prairie, Minnesota.

Books by
Leith Anderson

Becoming Friends With God
A Church for the 21st Century
Dying for Change
Leadership That Works
Praying to the God You Can Trust
Winning the Values War in a
Changing Culture

Elaine Larson

- faithful assistant
- valued colleague
- friend of God

CONTENTS

First Words 11

PART ONE: BEYOND ACQUAINTANCE 17

1. God Is Knowable 19
2. Who Jesus Is 28
3. Invitation to a Miracle 35
4. Twice Born................................... 42
5. Boastworthy Believers 49
6. Faith Matters 58

PART TWO: RELATIONAL RESPONSIBILITIES 65

7. What Is Prayer? 67
8. Teach Us to Pray.............................. 76
9. No Answer................................... 84
10. Response to a Message 93
11. Worthy of His Call 102
12. Pharisee and Publican 110

PART THREE: COMMUNICATION AND COMMUNION.............. 119

13. Loving Ourselves................................. 121
14. The Sharing Life 128
15. Imperfect People 134
16. Walking the Walk 142
17. Loving Our Neighbor............................ 150
18. Christ at Work................................... 156

PART FOUR: AMITY AND ENMITY 165

19. Holy and Separate.............................. 167
20. A Suffering World.............................. 175
21. The Hypocritical Christian...................... 184
22. Jesus and Satan 192
23. Possessed....................................... 200
24. The Way to Heaven 209
25. The Way to Hell............................... 217

PART FIVE: THE PERFECT FRIEND......................... 227

26. The Servant Lord 229
27. In the Presence of Glory....................... 236
28. The Gift of Peace 245
29. The Curing Touch 252
30. Born to Win 260
31. Loved by God 266

FIRST WORDS

Dear Friend,

Thank you for letting me call you friend. It is a special word. It speaks of a special relationship. Friendship is based on sharing something in common. The reason I think we are friends is that we both want to be friends with God.

When our daughter started school she wasn't concerned about the teacher, room number, or academic content—she just wanted to have a special friend in her class. It reminded me of my grade-school years—every June we received our classroom assignment for the next September and immediately compared assignments with our best friends to make sure we were all in the same homeroom. Friends are a most important part of life.

Unfortunately, not all of our friendships are lasting and satisfying. Friends move away. Friends can be fickle. Sometimes a friend dies and leaves a hole in our soul. Not even the best of friendships will ever be perfect.

I remember my wife's mother saying that when she was growing up she never really had a best friend until she met Jesus. Jesus became her

Savior and Lord, but he also became her friend. He is an extraordinary friend, better than any other. He's always there for us. He knows us better than anyone else. His friendship lasts beyond this life and into eternity. Jesus is God and there is nothing better than having God as your eternal friend.

The chapters ahead are about *becoming friends with God.* They are not intended to be a theology book, although they do present Christian truths. They are not intended to retell all the stories of the Bible, although they include lots of Bible stories. These pages unfold as our best friendships do—with ideas, stories, conversations, and a deepening relationship.

Our friendship with God begins by meeting him and getting to know him as a person. This is much more than knowing about God as we know about famous celebrities. Some of us feel like we are good buddies with politicians, musicians, movie stars, athletes, and television characters. We feel like friends because we've observed them from a distance. But they don't know us. Even if we've actually met one of them, it's unlikely that our name would be remembered or we would be counted as important in that celebrity's life. At most, this is not a friend but an acquaintance.

We want to be more than acquainted with God; we want to be best friends. That's why we begin at the beginning—Beyond Acquaintance. Here is the opportunity to be sure that you and I have a personal relationship with God that can deepen into a fulfilling friendship.

Once our friendship is firmly established we discover that all good relationships come with responsibilities—Relational Responsibilities. God has responsibilities to us and we have responsibilities to God. I suppose this could be compared with the watering, weeding, and fertilizing of a garden to make sure that the flowers and vegetables will grow strong. But relationships aren't like plants. We have to work and play to make a relationship all that it can be. If you have a lifelong friend from your growing-up years, you probably have grown that lasting friendship with long phone calls, exchanged birthday cards, and shared laughter, tears, parties, and tragedies. You both feel responsible to make the relationship strong, and that's the way it should be. Well, it's the same in our friendship with God—there are delightful and important relationship responsibilities that we don't want to neglect.

The third section to our friendship journey focuses on Communication and Communion, but let's be careful not to misunderstand. Friendships are not like mathematical formulas or the step-by-step assembly instructions that come with children's toys. Relationships have ups and downs, delights and difficulties, good days and bad days. That's why communication is so very important to every relationship. If we don't communicate on the same frequency, our friendship will never develop. In other words, communication is part of every day of our friendship with God—it's not like we get acquainted, learn our responsibilities, and then start communicating. They're all mixed up and blended together.

When communication gets wonderfully good, it becomes communion. Communion is like a connection of the souls. It's deeper and better and stronger than just about anything words can describe. The closest human examples are lifelong best friends, soul mates, identical twins, or the best of marriages. Actually, communion with God is more and better than all of these best examples put together. That's one of the reasons why becoming friends with God can and should be the most satisfying relationship of our lives.

Next to last in our talks together are pages about Amity and Enmity—the best and worst of what a friendship can become. Of course, we never want to have a falling-out with God that will strain and alienate our relationship. The good news is that we can have a supernatural love relationship with God that can endure everything from birth to death, victory to defeat, and happiness to horror. Only the very best and deepest friendships can survive and thrive through every circumstance of our lives.

Our last conversations focus on a lofty promise about the Perfect Friend. This description belongs to God alone. No matter how good it gets with a parent, child, husband, wife, neighbor, or teammate, none of them is perfect. Everyone will disappoint us more than once. And we all know how much it hurts to be disappointed by a friend. That's why we need God and that's why we want to be friends with God—he will never fail us, will never break up, will never be less than the best. No wonder we want God to be our very best friend.

Thank you again for sharing the journey. Read a chapter at a time. Read them all at once. Skip around. This book is not about the book . . . it is about becoming friends with God.

May your best friend be God himself!

Friends together with God,
Leith Anderson

*"Abraham believed God,
and it was credited to him as righteousness,"
and he was called God's friend.*

James 2:23

Part One

BEYOND
ACQUAINTANCE

❦

CHAPTER ONE

GOD IS KNOWABLE

God is great; God is good; God is holy; God is love—that is very good news if we personally know God. If we don't, then it isn't good news at all. This is not a minor matter. Actually it could not be more important, this whole business of knowing God.

The problem is that God is beyond our comprehension. The Bible says in Psalm 145:3, "Great is the Lord and most worthy of praise; his greatness no one can fathom." The greatness of God is deeper than the deepest ocean—it is beyond our ability to comprehend. Psalm 147:5 says, "Great is our Lord and mighty in power; his understanding has no limit." God is infinite; there is no limit to the understanding of God. But we are finite, we have all kinds of limits, and therefore we cannot fully comprehend him.

I remember when I brought our first computer home one Christmas. I set it up right there in the living room—the monitor, the keyboard, and the printer. It was a wonderful event! By today's standards that computer would be considered primitive. You had to put in the program that you wanted to use on very large floppy disks for there was no hard drive. Suppose you bought the latest Windows program on CD-ROM. When you tried to install it on that old computer, you'd find that there was no place to insert the CD-ROM. No matter what amount of money you'd spend to try to solve the problem, there would be no way for that simple computer to receive the information.

It is much the same way with us and with God. We are finite humans, and when we try to comprehend the infinite God, there just isn't a connection point. There is no way that information can be correctly installed in our minds, and even if there were, the vast amount of data about the personality, power, and presence of God is far beyond anything for which we have capacity. So a lifetime of trying would never make any difference. God is incomprehensible.

It is further explained in the New Testament:

> Oh, the depths of the riches of the wisdom and knowledge of God! How unsearchable his judgments, and his paths beyond tracing out! Who has known the mind of the Lord? Or who has been his counselor? Who has ever given to God, that God should repay him? For from him and through him and to him are all things. (Romans 11:33–36)

Another way of saying it is: God is the Creator and we are the creatures. He made everything including us. So that from him, and through him, and to him are all things. Everything. God is so much bigger, so much better, so much smarter, so much the Creator that we are unable to fully understand him. It would be like a painting trying to understand the painter, or a car trying to understand General Motors, or maybe a cloned sheep trying to understand the biologist. It's not going to happen.

God is in a different category than we are. God is the Creator; we are the creatures. He is so much higher that there is just no way for us to become like him. We can't know God unless God somehow makes himself known to us. If God will take the initiative, if God who is so much smarter and so much better and so much greater—if he would reach out to us in our ignorance, then we could know that he is great and good and that he is holy and loving. But if it were up to us, a million years of research would never tell us much of anything about God. The only way for us to know anything about God is for God to pass that information along to us.

The marvelous news is that he has. He has done this through three channels: creation, Jesus, and the Bible.

KNOW GOD THROUGH CREATION

Psalm 19:1 explains, "The heavens declare the glory of God; the skies proclaim the work of his hands." If we take a good look at the world around us—the galaxies, the heavens above us—we can learn a great deal about who God is as well as about what he has created. More detail is given in the New Testament. Romans 1:20 says, "Since the creation of the world God's invisible qualities—his eternal power and divine nature—have been clearly seen, being understood from what has been made." Paul is saying that we can look at creation and find out things about God that would otherwise be invisible. We can learn about and know about God through an exploration and study of what he has created.

Let's suppose that we have the drawings of three artists: on the left you have one of the works of Michelangelo, in the center a work by Picasso, and to the right one of the works of Charles Schulz. To the one extreme you have Michelangelo's *Moses* or *David* and to the other extreme you have Charles Schulz's Charlie Brown or Linus. If you just looked at the artwork and knew nothing about the artist, you could tell a lot. There is a big difference between Michelangelo and Picasso. You could tell that there is a huge difference between Michelangelo and

Charles Schulz. You would be able to tell invisible things about them from the artwork that they created.

We also can tell invisible things about God from the creation that we study and explore. Among the things that we can learn about are God's eternal power and his divine nature. But it is kind of a good news/bad news piece of information. For once we get this information, what will we do with it? It's not enough by itself.

It is a little bit like having some terrible disease and seeing on television that there is a clinic somewhere that has a therapy that will cure your disease. The problem is they never give the address. No matter who you call, no matter what you do, you can never get additional information. All you know is what you saw on television.

The information about God, the knowledge of God that comes through creation is good. It is wonderful, but it falls terribly short because it is simply intellectual knowledge and has no experiential benefit, no transforming power.

KNOW GOD THROUGH JESUS

But then comes Jesus. And that of course is what the Gospel—the Good News—is all about. John 1:18 says, "No one has ever seen God," but Jesus has made him known. Or Hebrews 1:1–2, "In the past God spoke to our forefathers through the prophets many times and in various ways, but in these last days he has spoken to us by his Son, whom he appointed heir of all things, and through whom he made the universe." God started out with nature and creation. He spoke through prophets who then passed his message along. But the apex, the best of all, is Jesus. He sent Jesus. Hebrews 1 explains that Jesus was the one through whom God the Father created the world in the first place, so there is a link. God's Son

But then comes Jesus.

is fully divine, so that when we hear Jesus, we hear God. When we experience Jesus, we experience God. When we learn about Jesus, it is God that we are learning about. God has become human so that we can know him.

It is like the botanist becoming a plant. God, in the person of Jesus Christ, became human so that we can know him. We're talking about the availability through Jesus of an eternal supernatural connection with God. Not just information at a distance, but close-up and personal and eternal.

We can have a relationship with Jesus Christ. A relationship as real, as personal, as intimate as with any other person, and even more so. But it is not with some distant person of ancient history, it is with Jesus who is alive today and is still God. We can, through faith, have a connection with him that is present and powerful; it is real and it is a means of knowing God—infinitely knowing God. Personally knowing God, and becoming friends with him.

KNOW GOD THROUGH THE BIBLE

The third way in which God has revealed himself is the Bible. The Bible is God's official record of his self-revelation throughout history. So the Bible explains something that we could not have otherwise experienced. In the beginning God created the heavens and the earth. God did it. He made the creation. But we weren't there, so he gave us a record so that we would know.

God spoke audibly to Moses and gave him the Ten Commandments. But we weren't there, we weren't even alive, so we have the record in the Bible. God sent his only Son to show us who God is and what God is like. He was born in Bethlehem, grew to maturity, and performed tremendous miracles. He lived a perfect life. He died on the cross to pay for human sin; he couldn't be kept down. He rose again to life. Except we weren't there. We have a record that comes from God so we can know.

Very near the end of the biography of Jesus, John wrote, "Jesus did many other miraculous signs in the presence of his disciples, which are not recorded in this book. But these are written that you may believe that Jesus is the Christ, the Son of God, and that by believing you may have life in his name" (John 20:30–31). These things are written so that we can have eternal life. God chose to reveal himself so that we could personally know him.

I realize that there are some who say, "As good as all that is, I wish that God would talk to me now the way he talked to people then. I see God in creation. I do love Jesus Christ as my Savior, and I do read the Bible, but there are times that I just don't know what to do. There are decisions I've got to make. I've asked God to actually talk to me out loud so that I would know for sure."

Sometimes we hear someone say, "God spoke to me."

You say, "Did he talk with you out loud?"

"No, he didn't say it out loud, but I'm sure it was God who actually talked to me."

And sometimes those who report new revelations from God, which are not in the Bible, claim these revelations are to be obeyed as surely as if they were written in the Bible. What are we supposed to think of that? How do we deal with that?

First of all, we need to be sure that God is the initiator. It is God who reveals himself to us. It is God who is the subject, and we are the object. So let us never imagine that simply because we want to hear something, God is therefore obligated to speak to us. When you read the accounts in the Bible of God's direct revelation to people, you see that many times they were caught completely by surprise. Young Samuel in the Old Testament had no idea who was talking. He had to go and ask someone else. It was God who took the initiative.

Let us be sure we understand our right place and our right relationship with God. It is God who is the revealer; it is God who is the initiator; it is God who then gives the information to us. It is based upon God's desire to speak more than it is based upon our desire to hear.

Certainly it is possible for people today to hear from God, but let us never think that it is on the same level as the revelation of God through his creation or through his Son or through his Scripture.

We must be very clear that we have sufficient revelation from God in what he has already given to us. We have 100 percent of everything we need to know in Jesus Christ and in the Bible. It is not as if God has left us hanging with some shortage of information. Anything that

It is God who reveals himself to us.

we are convinced is the will and the mind of God must be in accordance with the revelation of God that we already have. Martin Luther, the great reformer, spoke of *sola Scriptura*, or "the Bible alone," as our great authority.

THE ASTONISHING TRUTH

All of this leads to the astonishing truth that *we can know God.* It doesn't mean that we can know everything about God, for we cannot. We will never know everything about God because God is far greater than any capacity that we will ever have. But it is to say that we can personally know him. Not just about him, but we can know him. We can know God as God. We can know him as Savior. We can know him as Lord, as father, as friend.

Jesus prayed in John 17:3, "Now this is eternal life: that they may know you, the only true God, and Jesus Christ whom you have sent." That is to say that when we know God, we live forever with him. When we know God *as he wants to be known,* we believe God is who he presents himself to be. We believe that we are distanced from God by both our humanity and our sinfulness and that the connection to God is through Jesus Christ who came, and who died for us, and who rose again from the dead. And when we in faith believe all that to be true and claim it for ourselves, it is like installing the program in the computer—the connection is made! The sparks can fly. The power is there. It is then that we know God. The believing is called faith, the connecting is called salvation, and the result is eternal life.

Is this good? It is very good. But it is only the beginning. For we can spend the rest of our lives and the rest of eternity coming to know more and more and more about God and tightening the connection every moment, forever and ever. Think of how it is when you first meet a person, and after a short time you think, "Wow, I've really gained a lot of information." But the more you get to know the person, the more you discover what you didn't know. Getting to know God goes on and on and on. And it is more important than everything else that we would otherwise consider to be valuable in our lives!

There are some words worth memorizing in Jeremiah 9:23–24, where the Old Testament prophet says,

> "Let not the wise man boast of his wisdom or the strong man boast of his strength or the rich man boast of his riches, but let him who boasts boast about this: that he understands and knows me, that I am the Lord, who exercises kindness, justice and righteousness on earth, for in these I delight," declares the Lord.

The number one goal of our lives shouldn't be to get more wisdom, shouldn't be to get more wealth, shouldn't be to get greater strength. The best goal of all is to know God.

Once I was at a concert, and during the intermission, across the lobby, there was a famous national leader whom I had seen on television, but had never seen in the flesh. My host pointed this famous person out to me and said, "I know him."

I said, "You're kidding! You know him?"

"Yeah, I know him," he said. "Would you like me to introduce him to you?"

Now change the place from the concert hall to right here. Change the time from then to now. And change the famous person from the nationally known leader to God. You point to God and you say to me, "I know him."

I say, "You're kidding! You know him? You know God?"

You say to me, "Yeah. I really do. Would you like me to introduce him to you?"

God is great; God is good; God is holy; God is love; and God is knowable. You can know him. Really know him—through faith in Jesus Christ.

CHAPTER TWO

WHO JESUS IS

One of the most important conversations recorded in the Bible took place as Jesus and his disciples were walking through the suburbs of the city of Caesarea Philippi:

> Jesus and his disciples went on to the villages around Caesarea Philippi. On the way he asked them, "Who do people say I am?"
>
> They replied, "Some say John the Baptist; others say Elijah; and still others, one of the prophets."
>
> "But what about you?" he asked. "Who do you say I am?"
>
> Peter answered, "You are the Christ."
>
> Jesus warned them not to tell anyone about him. (Mark 8:27–30)

Jesus asked his first question in a most unlikely place for thirteen religious Jews to be walking. They were going to Jerusalem, and Caesarea Philippi was not on the way. Jesus must have really wanted to go there for him to take this rather circuitous route. The city was pagan. A temple had been built there to honor Caesar Augustus. Idolatry and paganism were essential to the economy of the community. But even before the time of Caesar, Greek mythology had said that Caesarea Philippi was where the Greek god Pan was born. Surrounded by all of this, Jesus turned and asked his disciples an unexpected question: "Who do others say that I am?"

Actually, it was a good place for him to ask that question. It's a question better asked in places secular than places sacred. Some people think that it's just a church question, that Jesus and discussions about him ought always be limited to a box that has a steeple on the top. But the truth is, Jesus spends far more time walking about and rubbing shoulders in the suburbs and the cities where the realities of idolatry and heathenism are practiced.

It is a most appropriate question, the kind of question that needs to be asked in school, or at work, where Jesus Christ's name is often mentioned. It seems as though no matter where you go, whether it is discussed intellectually as a religion, or spoken as profanity, or in casual seasonal conversation, people cannot seem to avoid talking about Jesus Christ. It may be more appropriate in the secular places than in the sacred places to ask the question, "Who do people say that Jesus is?"

The disciples had a quick answer. "Jesus, some say that you are John the Baptist, others say Elijah, and still others one of the prophets." It was an interesting list, because these men were all dead. It was somewhat like an ancient equivalent to the sightings of Elvis Presley or John F. Kennedy. They were saying that people had him confused with well-known dead people.

No matter where you go, people cannot seem to avoid discussion about Jesus Christ.

The first answer was that he was John the Baptist. A cousin of Jesus, John the Baptist was a fiery, bombastic preacher who named people as sinners and condemned them publicly for their sins. Baptist was not his denomination; he was called John the Baptizer because he called people to repentance, and when they repented he baptized them in a river. Baptism was a symbol of the cleansing they received from God as a result of their repentance.

A disconcerting practice of John was to call people out of the crowd by name and say, "You are guilty of [this sin or that sin]." In some ways it attracted a crowd, and in some ways it might have discouraged people from coming to listen to him! One that John named as a sinner was the king, Herod Antipas.

Maybe only if you are really into soap operas can you get all these connections, but let me try to explain. Herod Antipas, who was a grandson of the Herod in the Christmas story, had a niece named Herodias, who was married to his brother Philip, who also was a king in a nearby area. Herod Antipas decided that he wanted his niece for himself. So he divorced his wife and married his niece, who was also his sister-in-law. John the Baptist publicly condemned what he did and called his behavior immoral, incestuous, and illegal. King Herod Antipas responded by having John arrested and beheaded.

Some were saying that John had come back to life again under the name of Jesus.

Then others said, "No, he is Elijah." Elijah was the greatest miracle worker of the Old Testament, nine hundred years before the birth of Christ. He did spectacular miracles—even raising the dead back to life. He was extraordinary, and the last words of the Old Testament predicted that Elijah would come back again and prepare the way for the Messiah. So when people saw the miracles that Jesus did, they were astounded, and said, "Elijah is back."

Others said that Jesus was one of the prophets. Matthew, in his biography of Jesus, identifies this other prophet that they alleged to be as Jeremiah. Jeremiah was nicknamed "the weeping prophet," for he was a man of deep compassion and love who was heartbroken because the people rejected his message. Some people said that Jesus was Jeremiah: "Nobody listens to him, either, and he has such love, such compassion, such concern."

It is fascinating that the same Jesus could be seen so differently. Some people said, "He is one hellfire-and-brimstone preacher. He really lets them have it—just like John the Baptist." Others said, "No, no, he is like Elijah. Did you see the miracles? The next thing you know, he is going to be raising the dead. He's Elijah." And others said, "The main thing about him is his love and his compassion, his tenderness of heart, and his sensitivity."

They all saw different aspects. They all saw that Jesus was very special, but only human. Frankly, they saw him the way Muslims see him today. This conversation with Jesus is one of the great dividing points between Christianity and Islam. Islam teaches that Jesus was a great man, a miracle worker, a prophet, someone who helped to prepare the way for the greater later prophet, Muhammad.

WHO DO YOU SAY I AM?

Jesus then asked the second question, which was far more personal: "What about you? Who do you say I am?" It still is the question that divides Christians from Muslims, from Jews, from people of any other religion. His second question was to determine if he really made any difference in the lives of his disciples.

There were all kinds of crowds around Jesus, people who would hear what he had to say, who would discuss with one another the points that he made, but they weren't any different as a result. Jesus wanted them to understand that just hearing his words and hanging out in his crowd did not make a person his disciple. A Christian is someone whose life has been transformed by a relationship with Jesus Christ. She has different priorities. He has different morals. The person is changed so that sin is hated and Jesus is loved.

Jesus wanted to know, "What about you? Who do you say that I am?" Frankly, I find that uncomfortable, for it is much easier to talk in the third person about what other people have to say about Jesus. It is easier to talk about whether other people worship God or not, or whether they pray. It's more comfortable asking: "Do people really believe that God answers prayer? Do Christians forgive? If someone really hurts them and offends them, do you think they keep grudges at the same rate as others? What about giving? Are Christians significantly different from the rest of the population in terms of what they contribute?"

But it can get uncomfortably personal when the question is changed, and you're asked directly, "What do *you* think of Jesus? Do you love God? Do you forgive others? Do you pray? Do you give? Is your life changed?" Jesus asked them straight out if he had made a difference in their lives.

When he had thought it through, Peter gave a profound answer: "You are the Christ. Yes, Jesus, you are more than John the Baptist, the fiery preacher; you are more than Elijah, the spectacular miracle worker; you are more than Jeremiah, with all of his compassion and all of his tears. You are different, Jesus; you stand alone. You are one of a kind. You are the Christ, the Messiah, the anointed one from God."

Christ is a Greek word. The same word in Hebrew is *Messiah*, and the same word in English is *anointed one* or *chosen one of God*. But Peter's answer wasn't a technical or precisely theological answer. Oh, it was correct, but there was more to it than that. His answer was a commitment to Jesus' being the Christ, the Messiah, the anointed one. His answer acknowledged that who Jesus is makes a difference in the way a person lives life. For if Jesus is who he says he is, then he must be followed and he must be obeyed.

To be a Christian is the most radical and revolutionary change any person can have. It includes forgiveness of sin, the presence of God now, and the assurance of eternal life someday. But it also means living differently. Jesus sets the standard for how we live. A person who is a

Christian gives to Jesus his body, her money, one's entire life.

Peter said it all when he answered, "Jesus, you are the Christ."

Then Jesus said, "Don't tell anyone!" That's kind of a surprise. Aren't Christians supposed to share their faith with other people as far and fast as possible? But Jesus warned his disciples not to tell anyone about him.

Why? Because they didn't yet understand all that was involved. For being a Christian is a whole lot more than an insurance policy against hell. It's a whole lot more than an intellectual assent. It can be tough. It can be tougher than not being a Christian. It can include difficulty and pain and suffering.

Look at what Jesus said next.

To be a Christian is the most radical and revolutionary change that any person can have.

> Then he called the crowd to him along with his disciples and he said: "If anyone would come after me, he must deny himself and take up his cross and follow me. For whoever wants to save his life will lose it, but whoever loses his life for me and for the gospel, will save it. What good is it for a man to gain the whole world, yet forfeit his soul? Or what can a man give in exchange for his soul? If anyone is ashamed of me and my words in this adulterous and sinful generation, the Son of Man will be ashamed of him when he comes in his Father's glory with the holy angels" (Mark 8:34–38).

Being a Christian includes self-denial. It includes suffering, sacrifice, and an unashamed commitment to who Jesus the Christ really is. That runs counter to what most of us want to think. We are more prone to pleasure, to self-advancement, being a little bit embarrassed about Jesus when his name comes up—not this unashamed business.

There is an old legend about a wealthy, powerful emperor of the

Holy Roman Empire. They say that when he was buried they made the most extraordinary tomb for him. It was configured as a throne room and in it was deposited vast wealth: jewels, crowns, silver, and gold. It was beyond ordinary imagination. Those who buried him took his corpse and seated him on a throne with his elbow on the arm of the throne and his hand and finger holding up his head. They placed a Bible on his lap and sealed the tomb.

Centuries later, when archaeologists opened the tomb, they saw a somewhat different scene. As his body had turned to a skeleton, the hand fell and the finger pointed to Mark 8:36: "What good is it for a man to gain the whole world and yet forfeit his own soul?"

Peter said it before he fully understood it, but Jesus taught him what it meant to say, "Jesus, you are the Christ." Peter learned the lesson, and the rest of his biography says that he not only learned it, but he lived it, and that he died it as well. "You are the Christ."

Let me ask you that pointed, personal question that Jesus asked his disciples. "What about you? Who do you say that Jesus is?"

Understand what is involved when you say, *"Jesus, you are the Christ."*

CHAPTER THREE

INVITATION TO A MIRACLE

Recently I've been reading Sam Walton's autobiography. He was the founder of Wal-Mart, the largest retail outlet chain in the United States. He mentions all the downsides of his being named America's richest man. He tells about reporters coming to his house, even taking pictures of him with a telephoto lens while he was having his hair cut at a local barber shop. But the stupidest thing to him was the invitation he received to Elizabeth Taylor's wedding. He couldn't imagine why Elizabeth Taylor would invite a stranger from Bentonville, Arkansas, who drives a pickup truck with two bird dogs in the back, to her wedding in California.

You and I know why she invited him. Not because he was Sam Walton, but because he was labeled the richest man in America. Wedding invitations often say a lot. They say a lot both about who's invited and about who does the inviting. That's the way it was for the most famous wedding in history. It is not famous for the bride or groom (we don't even know their names), but it's famous for one of the invited guests. A man who was then and is now the richest man in the universe, although they didn't know that when they invited him to their wedding. The story is told in John 2:1–11.

> On the third day a wedding took place in Cana in Galilee. Jesus' mother was there, and Jesus and his disciples had also been invited to the wedding. When the wine was gone, Jesus' mother said to him, "They have no more wine."
>
> "Dear woman, why do you involve me?" Jesus replied. "My time has not yet come."
>
> His mother said to the servants, "Do whatever he tells you."
>
> Nearby stood six stone water jars, the kind used by the Jews for ceremonial washing, each holding from twenty to thirty gallons.
>
> Jesus said to the servants, "Fill the jars with water"; so they filled them to the brim.
>
> Then he told them, "Now draw some out and take it to the master of the banquet." They did so, and the master of the banquet tasted the water that had been turned into wine. He did not realize where it had come from, though the servants who had drawn the water knew. Then he called the bridegroom aside and said, "Everyone brings out the choice wine first and then the cheaper wine after the guests have had too much to drink; but you have saved the best till now."
>
> This, the first of his miraculous signs, Jesus performed at Cana in Galilee. He thus revealed his glory, and his disciples put their faith in him.

The wedding to which Jesus was invited was in a tiny village called Cana in the province of Galilee in what is Israel today. It wasn't far from Jesus' hometown of Nazareth. The family was probably poor—a safe guess because most families were poor then.

Weddings in those days were different from what we are used to. Betrothal (what we call engagement) began with solemn vows and lasted at least a year before the wedding. It was very serious stuff. It required a legal divorce to break the engagement.

The wedding itself was long—at least a day. It was on a Wednesday if the bride was a virgin, Thursday if she was a widow. The day of the wedding communicated whether the bride was a virgin much as a white wedding gown is meant to communicate virginity in modern times.

A grand feast that required an invitation preceded the wedding it-self, which took place after dark. After the wedding ceremony was over, there was a processional from house to house through the village and out into the countryside. The attendants carried a canopy over the bride and groom, and they stopped at every house to receive congratulations. It was part of the social custom of establishing their marriage within the broader community.

The procession ended at the couple's new home, where they began a week-long "honeymoon" to which everyone who came to the wedding was invited. That's somewhat different from the way we do it today! During those seven days, the bride and the groom were to be treated as if they were royalty, actually addressed as King and Queen. Their friends were supposed to cater to their every whim.

LET'S INVITE JESUS

What made this wedding most memorable took place back when the bride and groom and their families prepared their invitation list. Among all the other names of relatives and friends, someone said, "Let's invite Jesus of Nazareth." Perhaps someone else said, "But he's not even from Cana." Another said, "Let's invite him anyway." So they put his name on the list, and he made all the difference. The invitation and the inclusion of Jesus made this the most memorable and supernatural wedding of all of history.

The same is true for us. Our weddings and special events, if you count them in the course of all human activities, really are quite inconsequential. But what if we invite and include Jesus? Put the name of Jesus on the invitation list, add one more to the count for the caterer, set a place for him at the head table. Yes, invite Jesus, and expect him to come! It makes all the difference.

At the wedding in Cana they discovered that simply having Jesus there did not mean the absence of problems. The wedding celebration was going well, but then a problem arose. The wine ran out. They had hoped it would stretch. Maybe they guessed that some of the invited guests would not come. But they ran out, and it was embarrassing.

Hospitality was especially important in the Middle Eastern culture. Running short of wine could have been considered a breach of contract and resulted in a lawsuit. It sounds strange to us, but in those days if the host and hostess at a wedding feast invited you, and you accepted the invitation, and there were not adequate provisions, you could sue. This was a serious problem!

Mary, the mother of Jesus, was among the first to discover that they had run out of wine. She immediately went to Jesus. Up to this point in Jesus' life there is no record of his ever performing a miracle. So it wasn't that she expected a miracle. Maybe she thought that he would just say something that would relieve the tension.

Mary knew Jesus well after thirty years. She knew the kind of man that he was. She knew that he cared about people and was concerned about their problems.

I doubt that she understood when he said, "My time has not yet come." I don't think that she had a sense of the schedule that he was following from conception to crucifixion to resurrection and back to heaven again. She didn't understand all that. So when Jesus said what he said, she simply turned to the servants and said, "Well, just do whatever he says."

Mary was right. She got it. Her response teaches us a lot. Whenever problems arise, even if we've never seen Jesus do a miracle before, even when we don't understand Jesus' words and can't figure out how he will handle it—just take your problems to him and do whatever he says.

Nearby stood six stone water jugs, each with a capacity of twenty or thirty gallons. Jewish law dictated that everyone had to wash their hands before they ate, and so they had set aside lots of water. The very religious strict conservatives would actually wash their hands between every course of the meal. A lot of water would be used up. By this time the water pots were pretty much empty, and Jesus ordered the servants to refill them. As soon as they had filled them to the brim, Jesus told them to take some back out again and to serve it to the master of ceremonies.

The master of ceremonies had no idea what was going on. He had not heard any of these conversations and was not aware that they had run out of wine. He took what was poured out of the water jug, touched it to his lips, and knew it was wine. He knew wine well enough to recognize that it was perhaps the best quality wine he had ever tasted. He immediately went to the groom, took him aside, and said, "I've been to lots of weddings, and I know how it works. At the beginning of the feast the best wine is served. Then after people's palates have been desensitized, the cheap stuff comes out. But you have saved the best until last!"

Some fascinating facts come out of this wedding story. Fact number one: Jesus has supernatural power. He did a miracle here. He literally changed water to wine. Fact number two: When Jesus does something, he does it very well. It wasn't just wine, it was the best of wine! Fact number three: When Jesus does something special, he does it big. One hundred eighty gallons. That would have provided for a very large and a very long party!

When Jesus does something, he does it very well.

I like these facts because they say that we, too, can come to Jesus with our needs. We can take our embarrassing problems to the supernatural Jesus, who does what he does with excellence.

The story is about the wonder of what Jesus did. Look again at the epilogue. "This, the first of his miraculous signs, Jesus performed at Cana in Galilee. He thus revealed his glory, and his disciples put their faith in him."

Several years ago my wife, Charleen, and one of our children and I did something I've wanted to do for a long time. We went to northern Minnesota to visit the headwaters of the Mississippi River. We drove north through Bemidji and then on to Itasca State Park, and there it was—the beginning of the great Mississippi River. It isn't very big at that point—maybe twenty feet wide. I took the brave approach and walked across it on a very large log. Then I stepped back across from stone to stone and finally stepped into the twelve inches of water and waded the rest of the way across the bed of the Mississippi.

I read some of the statistics: The flow of the Mississippi is only a few cubic feet of water per second at the headwaters, but twenty-five-hundred miles later the Mississippi River flows into the Gulf of Mexico at the rate of almost a half-million cubic feet of water per second and is two *miles* wide at the mouth. It is an enormous change. Something that starts so small and ends up so huge.

As we were driving north, about twenty miles from the headwaters of the Mississippi we started to see signs every few miles pointing the way. You know, I didn't see anyone taking a picture of the signs. But when we actually got to Lake Itasca I was amazed at the number of people lined up to walk across, carrying their cameras and camcorders. Of course they weren't taking pictures of the signs. Who cares about the signs when you can see the real thing? The purpose of signs is to point people to the real thing.

Changing water to wine was a wonder, but only a sign pointing people to the real thing—the glory of God in Jesus Christ. The sign was there to point the way to faith. The sign revealed his glory and turned the disciples into persons of great faith.

Does Jesus do miracles today? Indeed he does. Some of them are large wonders like this and some of them are small. Some are common-place things woven into the fabric of our lives that we hardly even no-tice. But their primary purpose is not just to heal our diseases, solve our problems, or get us a job. Miracles then and now are signs—pointing to Jesus, showing us the way to faith.

Don't get all caught up with the signs. Be like the disciples and follow the signs to Jesus. Don't desire the signs for themselves, just use them to point your way to faith—to the real thing—to Jesus Christ.

CHAPTER FOUR

TWICE BORN

A man named Nicodemus followed the signs to Jesus and sought him out one night. His story is recorded in John's gospel.

> Now there was a man of the Pharisees named Nicodemus, a member of the Jewish ruling council. He came to Jesus at night and said, "Rabbi, we know you are a teacher who has come from God. For no one could perform the miraculous signs you are doing if God were not with him."
>
> In reply Jesus declared, "I tell you the truth, no one can see the kingdom of God unless he is born again."
>
> "How can a man be born when he is old?" Nicodemus asked. "Surely he cannot enter a second time into his mother's womb to be born!"
>
> Jesus answered, "I tell you the truth, no one can enter the kingdom of God unless he is born of water and the Spirit. Flesh gives birth to flesh, but the Spirit gives birth to spirit. You should not be surprised at my saying, 'You must be born again.' The

wind blows wherever it pleases. You hear its sound, but you cannot tell where it comes from or where it is going. So it is with everyone born of the Spirit."

"How can this be?" Nicodemus asked.

"You are Israel's teacher," said Jesus, "and do you not understand these things? I tell you the truth, we speak of what we know, and we testify to what we have seen, but still you people do not accept our testimony. I have spoken to you of earthly things and you do not believe; how then will you believe if I speak of heavenly things? No one has ever gone into heaven except the one who came from heaven—the Son of Man. Just as Moses lifted up the snake in the desert, so the Son of Man must be lifted up, that everyone who believes in him may have eternal life.

"For God so loved the world that he gave his one and only Son, that whoever believes in him shall not perish but have eternal life. For God did not send his Son into the world to condemn the world, but to save the world through him. Whoever believes in him is not condemned, but whoever does not believe stands condemned already because he has not believed in the name of God's one and only Son." (John 3:1–18)

Nicodemus was educated, powerful, and very religious. He had to be all three in order to be a member of the Sanhedrin, which was a body of seventy men that functioned as the supreme court of ancient Judaism. He was a Pharisee, which meant that he was one of the "separated ones." Pharisees had thousands of rules and regulations that touched upon almost every detail of life. The Pharisees were committed to keeping every one of the rules and kept themselves separate from those who weren't committed to keeping all the rules.

Yet Nicodemus was also a humble, God-seeking, and amazing man. When he came to Jesus, he called him *Rabbi*, which means teacher. Yet Jesus held no formal office as a rabbi or a teacher. Jesus didn't have the formal education that Nicodemus had. Jesus was an ordinary man, a carpenter from the rural area of a province called Galilee. But that isn't what counted to Nicodemus. What counted to Nicodemus was that in Jesus he saw God. He knew that God was there. He could hear it in the words Jesus said and the way he said them, and he could see it in the miracles—he knew that no one could ever do the miracles that Jesus did without the power of God.

I like Nicodemus. I like him and I want to be like him. I want to be the kind of person who isn't all that impressed with titles and formal education, not all that deferential just because someone has some position or some office. I want to be the kind of person, like Nicodemus, who can see beyond all that and is a seeker for God and is attracted to Jesus Christ.

In Jesus he saw God.

Some people have criticized Nicodemus: "If he is all that you have painted him to be, then why did he go see Jesus at night? Was he ashamed of something? Was he afraid he would be caught or embarrassed? Why didn't he go and talk to Jesus in the daylight and in public for everyone to see?" There are others, in his defense, who say that Jesus, surrounded by the crowd in the daytime, wouldn't have had time for the private conversation he shared late at night with Nicodemus. And Nicodemus was serious enough about Jesus and seeking enough for God that he wanted to have as much time as he could get in the privacy of a nighttime meeting.

What I find most interesting is that Jesus never mentions it—he neither criticizes nor defends the nighttime meeting. Jesus doesn't seem to care one way or the other when it is or where it is; what Jesus most cares about is that Nicodemus came. And that's the way Jesus feels about us. If we just come, it isn't the circumstances that count; it isn't the time of day or the degree of darkness or light of the place. What is important is that we are humble God seekers who come to Jesus Christ.

WHAT DO YOU MEAN, "BORN AGAIN"?

When Nicodemus came, Jesus wasted no time bringing up the heart of the matter. He said, "I tell you the truth, Nicodemus, no one can see the kingdom of God unless he is born again." And Nicodemus had no idea what he was talking about. It was not particularly connected with anything that had previously been said in conversation.

Jesus had an interesting teaching style. It was sometimes upsetting, perhaps even abrasive. Jesus would often make startling statements that people didn't understand. Sometimes they were radical and disturbing. And then once he had a person's attention, he would further explain until they could understand.

He knew where Nicodemus was coming from. He knew the man's heart. And my guess is that Nicodemus had in his heart a question that we've all asked when we're feeling depressed: "I wonder if I could start all over again? I wonder if I could just back up a few paces, erase everything I've said and done, and begin again? I wonder if there is some way I could just be born all over again? Is that possible? Is there some way to do that?"

Jesus had captured Nicodemus' attention and imagination, but when he said, "You are never going to see the kingdom of God unless you are born again," Nicodemus was confused. How does this work? Is Jesus talking about a person getting back inside his mother's womb and being born all over again?

Jesus explained that there are two births: earthly birth and heavenly birth. Earthly birth is the first one—it's what we've all experienced. It's the birthday we all celebrate once a year. But not everyone has experienced birth number two. That's the heavenly birth or the "above birth." Jesus was saying that the second birth is more important—not because it is number two, but because it is a birth from God. It is a ticket to heaven. It happens in a supernatural way, as if the Holy Spirit of God is the obstetrician that brings this transformation, this heavenly birth, into a person's life.

Even after Jesus said it all, Nicodemus struggled to understand. He was a smart man, an educated man, but he was having trouble with the theological theory of it all. Then Jesus said to him, "Nicodemus, *you* must be born again." There was an instant switch from the highly theoretical to the personal. It is, I suppose, the difference between sitting in a university classroom and hearing a lecture on heart transplants— from historical development to the latest technology—and sitting in a cardiologist's office having the doctor look you in the eye and say, "You must have a heart transplant if you are going to live." It becomes very personal at that point.

For Nicodemus, the theologian, the member of the Sanhedrin, the man with the education, it is a different matter when Jesus says, "Nicodemus, you personally must be born again."

It's the same thing with us. We can have our religious discussions and read the Bible and hear sermons and attend classes, but it's a different matter when one day we hear Jesus speaking our name, looking us in the eye, and saying, "*You* must be born again." Suddenly we switch from abstract theory to the very practical implementation, and then we ask what Nicodemus asked: "How can this be?" Jesus answered with something of an insult, at least it sounds like an insult to me. He is recorded as saying, in John 3:10, "Nicodemus, you are Israel's teacher, and you don't understand these things?"

One day we hear Jesus speaking our name and saying, "You must be born again."

In other words, "Come on, Nicodemus, this is the most important spiritual issue there is, and your job is to teach people about spiritual things. You're supposed to be able to explain to them about God, and yet you don't understand the most important thing that can happen in a person's life, the only basis for a permanent relationship with God? Nicodemus, that's your job—you're supposed to know about this."

But Nicodemus didn't know. Jesus makes a very important point—that this is a matter of heaven, and matters of heaven are not usually understood by those limited to the language of earth. Jesus explains that he alone knows both heaven and earth and speaks the language of both. Jesus alone is bilingual in the words of God and the words of humanity.

Jesus knew that Nicodemus would never understand a full and detailed description of the new birth. He knew that Nicodemus needed to experience it, and so he put it in terms that Nicodemus would understand. He said something like "Nicodemus, do you remember that time when the Hebrew people were sick and dying in the desert of an awful plague and there was nothing that could be done? God told Moses to put a pole in the ground and then to hang a brass snake on the pole and to spread the word for everybody to look up at the snake, and when they did, they were healed. Do you remember that story, Nicodemus? Just like that, Jesus, the Son of Man, will also be put up on a cross, and those who look up to him will be saved from sin and death. They will enter the kingdom of God; they will be born from above."

But how does that work? How does just looking at Jesus—believing in him—how does that transform someone's life for now and forever? Jesus further explained:

> For God so loved the world that he gave his one and only Son, that whoever believes in him shall not perish but have eternal life. For God did not send his Son into the world to condemn the world, but to save the world through him. Whoever believes in him is not condemned, but whoever does not believe stands condemned already because he has not believed in the name of God's one and only Son. (John 3:16–18)

Jesus seemed to ask, "Nicodemus, do you understand that much? Do you understand that God loves us enough to send his Son Jesus to make a new-birth offer? Do you understand that if we believe, we are born again and not condemned? If we don't believe, we're stuck with the first birth and we're condemned, and condemned means hell."

Let's do what Jesus did, and that is to personalize all of this. In Jesus' words, you must be born again—because if you're not, then you are limited to your earthly birth. If you're not born again, then your sins aren't forgiven, you're not a citizen of heaven, you can't call God your friend, and you'll never enter his kingdom.

So just do it. Just look to Jesus and believe. Believe Jesus died for your sins and ask him for the new birth.

CHAPTER FIVE

BOASTWORTHY BELIEVERS

Boasting is bad, or at least that is what we usually think. We consider it to be socially unacceptable for someone to say how great he is, how much money she makes, how important his job is, or what connections and friendships she may have.

What is true in our society was pretty much the same in the first century. That is why the apostle Paul was reluctant to brag about the churches he had founded. It might sound as if he was taking the credit, and that just wasn't the way things were done. But then along came those Thessalonians, and he thought them so terrific that he had to boast. He was so thankful for them and so proud of them. As he spoke to other churches he just had to tell them how great the Thessalonians were.

How do we compare to those Thessalonians? Would we also be classified as boastworthy believers? Are we sufficiently terrific in our Christian lives that he could brag about us? If not, shouldn't our goal and desire be to be the kind of Christians who are elevated as models to other people?

In 2 Thessalonians 1:1–4 are three characteristics of boastworthy believers. Paul wrote this letter no more than six months after the first letter to the Thessalonians—both in A.D. 51.

> Paul, Silas and Timothy,
> To the church of the Thessalonians in God our Father and the Lord Jesus Christ:
> Grace and peace to you from God the Father and the Lord Jesus Christ.
> We ought always to thank God for you, brothers, and rightly so, because your faith is growing more and more, and the love every one of you has for each other is increasing. Therefore, among God's churches we boast about your perseverance and faith in all the persecutions and trials that you are enduring.

BOASTWORTHY BELIEVERS GROW IN FAITH

The first characteristic is growing faith. Paul boasts that the Thessalonians have faith that is "growing more and more." But it was not always that way. There was a time when they had no faith. They weren't even Christians! Paul reflects upon it in his first letter to them, saying that there was a day when "you welcomed the message with the joy given by the Holy Spirit. . . . You turned to God from idols to serve the living and true God, and to wait for his Son from heaven, whom he raised from the dead—Jesus, who rescues us from the coming wrath" (1 Thessalonians 1:6, 9–10).

There is an important truth here. At one point in time the Thessalonians were not believers and at another point in time they were. The implication is that we cannot grow faith until we have faith. Imagine trying to grow vegetables in a garden that has not first been seeded. It would be an exercise in futility to go to the garden every day and water and fertilize and chase the rabbits away in the hope of growing carrots, if you had never planted a seed. In order for something to grow, it must first begin. For a friendship to grow, we must first meet the individual, whether in person or through some means of communication.

The same goes for faith. Unless someone first becomes a Christian, there is no faith to grow. Many people in America are fooled into thinking they are Christians simply because they attend church a few times a year. That is like thinking you are a car because you're in a garage! Becoming a Christian is based on personal faith. It is believing in Jesus Christ as Savior and Lord. You have to do it yourself!

Probably you have done that. Many can point back to some calendar date and say, "That is the time when I, like the Thessalonians, received the message with joy. The day before I could not be counted as a believer, but on that day I came to faith in Jesus Christ." There is no point in talking about growing faith if, in fact, there is not initial faith. There must be a beginning in order for faith to grow. Each of us must answer Jesus' question, "Who do *you* say that I am?" and, as Nicodemus learned, have a second—heavenly—birth.

When some people become Christians, they grow quickly, like the beanstalk in the children's story. The seed of faith germinates and sprouts with great vigor and wonder. Then sometimes growth stalls or plateaus, or maybe it even decreases. Instead of a growing faith, it is a shrinking faith.

That is apparently the way it was for at least some of those Thessalonians. Paul worried about them. In his first letter he sensed that something was missing and their faith was not growing as it should grow. He wrote, "Night and day we pray most earnestly that we may see you again and supply what is lacking in your faith" (1 Thessalonians 3:10).

Have you had a car that stalled occasionally? Did you know frustration while driving it? Some years ago our family had a Ford station wagon that ought to be in the *Guinness Book of World Records* for stalling out. It stalled on an average of once every mile on a trip from

New Jersey to Colorado—that's about two thousand stalls! I think we went to every Ford dealership between the East Coast and the Rocky Mountains, and no one ever found out what was the matter with the car. But something was wrong.

Some Christians are like that Ford. Something's wrong, and they stall all the time. One minute they believe and the next they don't. It is difficult to grow when there is a constant uncertainty and irregularity to Christian faith.

Paul's prayer in his first letter to the Thessalonians was answered by the time he wrote his second letter to them. That is why I believe it was with great delight that he wrote, "Your faith is growing more and more." It makes me want to figure out how that change took place. How did those who were not believers, and who became believers and were then stalling out, get to the point that Paul described them as boastworthy Christians who were "growing more and more"?

We ought to be able to measure the growth in our faith over the last six months or year.

I see two divinely given factors here: one is circumstance and the other is choice. God initiates or allows a multitude of circumstances in our lives, each of which precipitates a choice of whether to trust God or not. The circumstances come in every color, shape, and size. For some, it is ill health. For others it may be depression, job loss, or unpaid bills. Some experience one long and protracted crisis, while others experience a whole series, one crisis after another. But every one of these circumstances gives us the choice of dealing with them in our own sputtering resources or in faith, by trusting in God in a way that we have not previously trusted him. And when we trust him, then we become the kind of boastworthy believers who are growing in faith.

We all agree that height is measurable, but we may doubt that faith is measurable. Yet Paul apparently thought that over a six-month period it was possible to measure an increase in faith. He was able to look at where the Thessalonians were, and then six months later look again and see where they had come. That challenges me to think that we ought also to be able to measure the growth in our faith over the last six months or year.

BOASTWORTHY BELIEVERS LOVE

The second characteristic of a boastworthy believer is increasing love. Just as Paul was concerned earlier about the Thessalonians' faith, he was also concerned about their love. Faith and love are the twin ingredients for the identification of Christians. If we have neither faith nor love, then we can't say that we are followers of Jesus Christ.

In his first letter Paul had prayed, "May the Lord make your love increase and overflow for each other and for everyone else" (1 Thessalonians 3:12). Again he was measuring where they were. The Thessalonians were very new Christians. They had had only a few weeks of instruction in the Christian faith. I sense that there were evidences of love, but inadequacy too, in the love they expressed to each other.

I know there were doctrinal differences within the church, particularly over the timing and the character of the second coming of Jesus Christ. As a result of that, some had quit their jobs and sold their homes and were waiting outside for Jesus Christ to come back. That had created tension because they had run out of money and others in the church had to work to provide the money for those who refused to work. And then, of course, there were the inevitable differences that come whenever you put people together. But when Paul observed all of the interpersonal relationships, he came to the conclusion that they must *increase* their love for each other and for everyone else. So my guess is that there were some people in the church of Thessalonica who were kind and some who were not. Some built up the others and some put others down. Some were forgiving and others held grudges. Love was there but it needed to grow.

Six months later there was marked improvement, and he wrote to them again saying, "The love every one of you has for each other is increasing" (2 Thessalonians 1:3). Not that they had arrived, for their love was far from perfect, but they had increased in love. There was measurable and observable change.

*Every single believer
in that church
had increased
in love!*

Every single believer in that church in Thessalonica had increased in love! Paul had to be thinking of specific individuals. Perhaps there was a woman who always held grudges who decided to forgive. There might have been two men who wouldn't talk to each other, who had gotten into some type of relational deadlock, but somehow in that six-month period one of them took the first step and broke the deadlock. Or maybe families who were at odds with each other started getting along, or people in debt to each other made strides to start paying back what was owed. It was enough to make Paul look at them all and say, "You are increasing in love." It was something worth boasting about.

And how about us? Are we the kind of boastworthy believers who are increasing in love? I'm not suggesting perfection, for I know myself and others too well to even hint at it. But I can take delight in the real possibility that we can increase in love in those simple things of forgiveness, of paying back money, of helping someone out financially, and of building relationships between people. We can do it, so that six months from now, if Paul or another outside observer were to look at our lives and measurement could be made, it could be clearly boasted that we, because of Jesus Christ, had increased in our love.

BOASTWORTHY BELIEVERS PERSEVERE

A third characteristic of boastworthy believers is ongoing persever-ance. This spiritual growth wasn't taking place in easy times. These people in Thessalonica were really up against it with persecutions and trials. Their growing faith and increasing love were against a backdrop of severe difficulty.

Maybe that is not surprising. For do you not find in your walk with Jesus Christ that when things go well there seems to be a time of spiritual plateau, but when problems come you are more likely to increase your faith? These people were under persecution. The Greek word Paul uses means an external attack.

Historians tell us that Thessalonica became one of the leading cities for persecution against believers. The governor ordered worship of Caesar. The Christians said that they had only one God and they could not worship anyone in the pagan pantheon nor could they wor-ship a living man such as Caesar. And so they refused. Someone con-cocted the idea of dedicating wine in the pagan temples either to Caesar or to Venus and then bringing that wine to the marketplace and sprinkling it on all of the produce, claiming it was dedicated to Caesar or Venus. Then the Christians couldn't buy food. Their diffi-culties increased until they couldn't get jobs or ply their own trades. Later at Thessalonica, Christians were burned and crucified.

While we may not face that kind of persecution, some of us may be discriminated against in our jobs, schools, or families because of our friendship with Jesus Christ. We need to remember that when the Thessalonian Christians were persecuted, they grew in their faith and increased in their love. Tough times can be growth times.

There was another side to the difficulties they faced. We're told in 2 Thessalonians 1:4 that the persecutions were accompanied by trials. While persecution was external, trials were the everyday pressures they had to face. Trials are the ongoing hassles that everyone faces.

The Christians in Thessalonica faced trials as we do and yet they grew in faith and increased in love. They may have had severe persecution and been pressed in by all kinds of trials, but responded with perseverance and faith. They didn't quit. The particular Greek word that is translated *perseverance* means more than survival or just hanging in there. It's a more positive response—a creative response. It's saying that even though adversity might be great, trust will be greater so that one can grow spiritually through the tough times.

> *Tough times can be*
> *growth times.*

I want to be very careful here. I don't want to glibly say, "Hey, I know you're really up against the wall with tough things in life, but just look at the positive side. The Christian way is to rise above the problem," and then walk away. To do that is a disservice. Seldom does that kind of advice change how anyone copes with the persecutions or trials of life. Perseverance is a perspective that genuinely trusts God through the worst of times, and that trusting of God is what then precipitates the growth in faith and the increase in love.

Warren Wiersbe says, "God never wastes suffering." I like that . . . and I believe that. God never wastes persecution, trials, hassles, or problems, but he always uses them for good in our lives. When we have that perspective, then we can also have the type of perseverance and faith that can creatively and positively respond to the difficulties that we are up against.

When I read the opening words of Paul's second letter to Thessalonica, I think about you who are reading this book. I have no difficulty boasting about your growing faith, your increasing love, and your ongoing perseverance. But I'm not sure I can say "everyone." It worries me a little when we talk about boastworthy believers—and Paul used the word "everyone." My concern is that perhaps not everyone reading these words could be described as growing in faith, increasing in love and perseverance. So that becomes my dream.

May each of us be boastworthy believers: growing in faith, increasing in love and in perseverance.

CHAPTER SIX

FAITH MATTERS

A centurion was a noncommissioned officer in the Roman army. The Roman army was divided into legions, with six thousand soldiers in each, and legions were subdivided into centuries of one hundred men each. Over each century was a centurion. It was a career position, and history says the centurions were very good at what they did. In wars they led the men into battle rather than retreat to some command post. They were courageous, willing to lay down their lives. In peacetime they were responsible for the discipline, training, and morale of the Roman soldiers.

Centurions were good men, the stalwarts, the backbone not only of the army but also of much of the structure of the Roman Empire. In fact, we find several centurions mentioned in the New Testament. At Calvary it was a centurion who stood by the cross when Jesus died and looked into his face after his death and said, "Surely this man was the Son of God." A few pages later in the New Testament, it was a centurion named Cornelius who was the first Gentile to become a Christian.

We turn some more pages to the biography of Paul and find him in one dilemma after another. He was chased, his life was being threatened, he was arrested, and he was hauled off to Rome for an appeal to Caesar. Often he was rescued by Roman centurions. They were good men.

As we read these stories we discover that, without exception, the New Testament reports the stories of these centurions positively and with honor. But understand also that centurions were Gentiles. Ancient Jews didn't like Gentiles, especially Romans, and more especially soldiers, for the Roman armies had conquered the land that God had given to their ancestors before them. No practicing religious Jew would ever step inside a Gentile's house. Especially a rabbi. It was against the law. Not only that, but in most cases a truly devout Jew wouldn't even speak to a Gentile.

It borders on amazing that Jesus, the rabbi, conversed with a centurion as he did. Matthew's transcript is worth reading.

> When Jesus had entered Capernaum, a centurion came to him, asking for help. "Lord," he said, "my servant lies at home paralyzed and in terrible suffering."
>
> Jesus said to him, "I will go and heal him."
>
> The centurion replied, "Lord, I do not deserve to have you come under my roof. But just say the word, and my servant will be healed. For I myself am a man under authority, with soldiers under me. I tell this one, 'Go,' and he goes; and that one, 'Come,' and he comes. I say to my servant, 'Do this,' and he does it."
>
> When Jesus heard this, he was astonished and said to those following him, "I tell you the truth, I have not found anyone in Israel with such great faith. I say to you that many will come from the east and the west, and will take their places at the feast with Abraham, Isaac and Jacob in the kingdom of heaven. But the subjects of the kingdom will be thrown outside, into the darkness, where there will be weeping and gnashing of teeth."

Then Jesus said to the centurion, "Go! It will be done just as you believed it would." And his servant was healed at that very hour. (Matthew 8:5–13)

The centurion was concerned about a servant of his who was paralyzed and in pain. Let's call this servant what he really was—a slave (same Greek word). He was a slave at a time when slavery was common, although we sometimes forget that slavery takes place today as well.

Slavery is an inhumane, despicable, and immoral practice where one human being owns another. Under Roman law a slave owner could do absolutely anything to a slave. A slave was considered to be a piece of property. He could rape a slave. He could torture a slave. He could sell a slave. He could work a slave to death. As long as it was his slave, it didn't make any difference. He could do anything at all. The extent of the cruelty in some cases was unbelievable.

But apparently this centurion was different. He cared. He had compassion for someone that typically no one had compassion for. I'm sure that he would feel uncomfortable if he heard me use the word love, but I think he loved this slave and was willing to do something quite humbling. As a Roman officer and a Gentile, he was willing to go to a Jewish rabbi and seek help. What would the other officers think? What about the hundred men under his command? If they heard about it, they might consider him a contemptible person for condescending to deal with the Jews of the land. They might refuse to obey his orders because of it. He set all that aside because of compassion—because he cared.

He went to Jesus and said, "Lord, my servant lies at home paralyzed and in terrible suffering." Interesting that he did not ask Jesus to heal him. He simply stated the need. Jesus' response was simple: "I will go and heal him."

The centurion came back with an amazing answer. "Lord, I don't deserve to have you come under my roof. Let me tell you how I see things. When I say a word, something happens; I'm obeyed. I can say to one of my men, 'Go,' and he goes. To another one, 'Hey, come here,' and he comes. I can say to one of my slaves, 'Do this,' and he does it. So you can just speak a word and my servant will be healed."

He was using an analogy to communicate his conviction that all was under the authority of Jesus—absolutely everything. He believed that when Jesus spoke, all must obey. He believed that everything was subject to Jesus' authority. He believed that the sick could be made well. He believed that marriages were under the authority of Jesus. He believed that Jesus had the ultimate control over the politics of the empire. He was convinced that religious matters and matters of economics, of employment and unemployment, that outcomes of battles, that every single detail, all things in life are under the authority of this Jesus.

This centurion would say that Jesus could do anything. Every detail of our lives, the things that trouble us, the things we get stressed out over, everything is under the authority of Jesus. Which means that Jesus need only speak a word and that sick servant would be

He believed that all was under the authority of Jesus—absolutely everything.

healed. It is not necessary for Jesus to go see him or to touch him. He just has to say it and it will happen. For after all, the centurion must have thought, this Jesus was God.

AN ASTONISHING FAITH

Matthew tells us that Jesus was *astonished* at the centurion's words. Jesus said, "I tell you the truth, I have not found anyone in Israel with such great faith." He would have expected it to be the other way around. This Roman centurion was from a pagan religious and cultural tradition. He should have been the last person to figure out what makes the universe work. Yet he understood things that those who were religious did not understand.

Life is full of such surprises. For example, research shows that in our society, the less money people have, the higher percentage of their income they give either to God or to charity, and that the more money people have, the lower the percentage they give. You would think it would be the other way around. Another surprise is that some of the greatest stories of faith in God and stories of the biggest miracles happening today are in Africa, Latin America, and parts of Asia. You would think they'd come out of Europe, where the Bible has been taught and the church has been established for centuries. Likewise, there are people who have grown up in Christian homes, have gone to Sunday school, church camps, and confirmation, and they never get it; they never understand what makes life work or how God operates. Then along comes somebody with none of that background, none of that tradition, none of that teaching, and he sees it. He understands it and his life is transformed and is completely different.

Jesus was saying, it was an astonishing thing for a Roman soldier to have more faith in Jesus than any Jew in Israel. After that dialogue with the centurion, Jesus switched to a monologue where he taught a powerful and profound truth to his disciples.

He began by teaching that faith is what counts. Faith is the key to understanding both life and eternity. At that time the Jewish people thought of heaven as a huge feast. God would be the host at the head table and the patriarchs of the Hebrew nation—Abraham, Isaac, and Jacob—would be seated with him. They also thought that the only people who were invited to that feast and to heaven were Jews, and everybody else was left out.

That was the way most Jews figured heaven would be. Jews were included and everybody else was left behind to scream, weep, and gnash their teeth. But Jesus taught a completely different truth. He said that at the banquet table called heaven there will be people from everywhere.

"I say to you that many will come from the east and the west, and will take their places at the feast with Abraham, Isaac and Jacob in the kingdom of heaven" (Matthew 8:11). He was saying that heaven will be filled with people from the east: from Iran, Iraq, Persia, India, China, and Japan. And from the west: from throughout the Roman Empire and across Europe and Africa. Millions of people who are not Jews will be included, eventually stretching all the way to the then-unknown Western Hemisphere that we call the Americas. Millions and millions will be at God's banquet table—not because they are Jews or Gentiles or black or brown or white or yellow, but *the* determining factor is faith.

Jesus is teaching that the basis for getting into heaven is faith—nothing else. One must believe that Jesus Christ has authority over all of life. He has the authority to forgive sin, and he alone has the authority to grant a guaranteed place in heaven.

That was a stunning teaching for those ancient people. Then he stunned them even more by adding that some who were Jews, who thought they had a guaranteed place, would be excluded if they lacked faith. "But the subjects of the kingdom will be thrown outside, into the darkness, where there will be weeping and gnashing of teeth" (Matthew 8:12).

It's common for people to think they are guaranteed a place in heaven because of their background.

You see, it was common in those days to believe that just because of your background, heaven was a sure thing for you. Jesus was saying that is not so. No faith, no heaven.

It's common today for people to think they are guaranteed a place in heaven because of their background. When you ask people if they expect to go to heaven, they say, "Sure, I'm a Baptist, I'm a Catholic . . . a Presbyterian."

Many of us work in companies that have central computer systems. One of the things we do when we get to work is to log on to the system.

We sit at the keyboard and enter our name and a password. We must spell our name right and get the password exactly right. It can't be off even one letter, otherwise there is no access.

Jesus is telling us to think of heaven pretty much the same way. To get into heaven we must state our name and the password, and no other password will work. The password is "faith." It can't be just any faith, it must be faith in Jesus Christ as Savior and Lord. When Jesus first taught this, some of those people must have been absolutely shocked. They had never heard anything like this before. It meant they were flirting with eternal death as a result.

Each of us needs to get it straight, as it could not be more important. Access to heaven is only by faith in Jesus Christ. It's a faith that needs to be registered in advance. We must tell God that we have faith in his Son, so that the record is there before we arrive.

The story ends with a wonderful epilogue. Jesus tells the centurion with faith that his request has been granted, that Jesus has already made the sick servant well. So the officer goes back home and finds the servant healed. He asks what time he recovered and confirms that it was the same hour that Jesus spoke the word. There was no doubt in his mind that Jesus was the one who had done it.

When we have this confidence, this trust, this faith in Jesus Christ, it will always show results. Jesus always makes a significant difference in the lives of those with faith.

Part Two

—

RELATIONAL
RESPONSIBILITIES

CHAPTER SEVEN

WHAT IS PRAYER?

What is prayer? It is a simple question and deserves a simple answer, but I have trouble finding a simple answer. I took out a yellow legal pad and a pencil and picked the dictionary off the shelf next to my desk and found, for me, a wholly inadequate answer. Then I took some more books off the shelf, but I really couldn't find anything particularly satisfying.

I know prayer is essential to our relationship—our friendship—with God. I also know that prayer is more than asking. It includes adoration and worship, confession, meditation, submission, intercession for other people, thanksgiving, and much more. I decided that defining prayer is somewhat like defining love. It is better defined by experience than by words. So I gave it my best shot and came up with a short definition: Prayer is communion with God.

I started out thinking that prayer is communication with God. That certainly is true, but prayer is much more than that. When you call a friend on the phone and get his answering machine because he isn't home, the message you leave is communication but hardly "communion." Prayer is communion with God. I don't mean the sacrament of bread and wine, but the sense of intimacy in a close relationship. It's the communication between a mother and a baby who is nursing at her breast. It's the communion or the communication between two people who are the very best of friends. It's the dynamic between a man and a woman who are in love.

That's what prayer is. It is communion with God and sharing a relationship with God himself. Saint Augustine wrote, "True prayer is nothing but love."

Christians are those who are related to God through Jesus Christ, and prayer is both the introduction to that relationship and the basis of the maintenance of that relationship. It is a love communion with God himself where he first loves us and then we love him. While admittedly at times we drift away and sin, yet there is a pull that is stronger than gravity that sucks us back to him. Then we are called upon to confess our sins with the guarantee in advance that our relationship will be fully restored and we will be forgiven. It is a communion in which we can share with him the deepest secrets of our hearts, known to no other. God alone truly understands us. He shares the heights of our joys and the depths of our sorrows.

Prayer is the language of the soul as it talks to God.

Prayer is an intimate connectedness with God. It is the language of the soul as it talks to God and hears him in return. Prayer is sharing this relationship in words; sometimes in thoughts, sometimes in songs, sometimes in silence. Prayer is the language of the soul communicating with God himself.

There is so much to be said about prayer. When you read the Bible you find prayer is like a thread woven through every book and almost every story. Over the last two thousand years thousands of books have been written on the subject of prayer, and they have not begun to exhaust all that can be said and understood. But when it comes to the basics, to the essentials of prayer, we must go back to Jesus Christ. For to be a Christian is to pattern one's life after Jesus, and to pray is to pray as Jesus prayed.

TO PRAY AS JESUS PRAYED

From the beginning of his public ministry, prayer characterized Jesus' life. For example, Luke 3:21 describes crowds of people being baptized in the Jordan River by John, Jesus' cousin. Just as Jesus calls us to be baptized in order to identify with him, he chose to be identified with us in baptism. John was reluctant. Although he had baptized hundreds of other people, it seemed inappropriate to baptize Jesus; but Jesus insisted, and so there in the Jordan River, John baptized Jesus. As Jesus was being baptized, we are told that he prayed. He wasn't thinking about the temperature or the depth of the water, or what the other people were thinking, or how he looked. Throughout the entire experience of baptism Jesus was praying and communing with God. A stunning thing happened: "As he was praying, heaven was opened and the Holy Spirit descended on him in bodily form like a dove. And a voice came from heaven: 'You are my Son, whom I love; with you I am well pleased' " (Luke 3:21–22).

That's what prayer is. It is the key that opens up heaven. Prayer touches the heart of God. Prayer is two-way communion of love and relationship. We have no record of what Jesus said in his prayer—perhaps it was too private for us to know. What is important is that he prayed. And so for us who pattern our lives and our prayers after Christ, prayer is love communion with God—the key that unlocks heaven.

But that was just the beginning. Just as people today love to know about the private lives of the rich and famous, people have always been curious about the life of Jesus. Mark gives a fascinating insight into

Jesus' private life. He says, "Very early in the morning, while it was still dark, Jesus got up, left the house and went off to a solitary place, where he prayed" (Mark 1:35).

This is an especially amazing declaration in light of how Jesus spent the day before. Read the rest of the first chapter of Mark, and you'll discover that the previous day he had preached to crowds in the synagogue, expelled a demon from a hostile man, and was constantly pursued by people seeking his attention. The word had spread that Jesus was in town, and although he had been physically and spiritually drained and was seeking rest in a private home, the people still came, wanting their questions answered, wanting to be healed, wanting to see and touch him. When he went to bed that night he must have been absolutely exhausted. Then early the next morning, before dawn, after that kind of a day, he got up and went to a solitary place in order to pray.

We sometimes think of Jesus in his humanity as somehow stronger than we are, but that is a false assumption. He got tired as we do; he had emotions as we have emotions; and when his days were long and he was tired, it was hard for him to get up the next day.

I try to understand a little bit of what Jesus faced although I have never faced a day quite like his. I preach several times on Sunday mornings, and that for me is a draining experience. By noon on Sunday I am not good for much of anything. It's as if I've done a week's work. I'm tired out.

Like Jesus, you and I have been confronted by difficult people, people who are in our face, yelling at us, people who are full of evil, and it is as if we are dealing with the devil in person. And even if we come out okay, we can hardly move or talk after that kind of ordeal. We understand with Jesus what it is like to have one of those awful, memorable days of dealing with children, parents, sickness, or difficulties at work—until by the end of the day we just plop on the bed wondering what more could happen.

When Jesus got up the next morning, I'm sure it was not an easy thing for him to do. When he went to pray, I suspect that he was drowsy at best. I might go so far as to think that when he prayed, some of his sentences were never finished because he dozed off, simply from the exhaustion of the day.

I'm not suggesting that when we have our difficult days we need to set the alarm before dawn, nor that there is anything more virtuous about praying before the sun rises. But if as Christians we are to pattern our lives after Christ, then prayer is also a priority for us.

Luke 5:16 tells us that after a draining and busy day, "Jesus often withdrew to lonely places and prayed." Jesus gave priority to privacy in his prayer life. Not that he didn't pray in public, because he did. A number of his public prayers are recorded in the Bible. But it's almost as if the prayers of Jesus were like an iceberg with only the small tip showing above the surface, while there was this huge understructure down below that was private. No one could see it, yet it supported what could be seen. All the miracles he did, all the knowledge and resources God provided for him—all of that was based not upon what happened in public but upon what happened in private.

If we are to pattern our lives after Christ, then prayer is also a priority for us.

When his followers came and asked him, "How are we supposed to pray? Teach us to pray," Jesus said, "When you pray, go into your room, close the door and pray to your Father, who is unseen. Then your Father, who sees what is done in secret, will reward you" (Matthew 6:6).

Jesus' private relationship with God fueled his life in public. That's the pattern for us to follow. The combination of the priority and the privacy of prayer gives the best of relationships with God and fuels us for everything else in our lives.

In Luke 6:12 there is a fourth insight into Jesus' practice of prayer.

It tells about when he made an extremely important decision, perhaps one of the most important of his entire career. It was the day when he picked his disciples—the ones who would communicate his message to the rest of the world and to future generations. On that day he wisely chose Matthew, who wrote his biography, along with Peter, who would make the insightful declaration that "you are the Christ" and would write part of the New Testament as well. He chose John, another of his biographers, and Thomas, who would first appear to be the ultimate doubter, but eventually would become the apostle to India. What's amazing is that before Jesus made this important decision, he spent the entire night in prayer. He went out to a mountainside and spent the night praying to God, and when morning came he called his disciples to him and chose twelve of them.

That's what Christians are to do—pray significantly before making big, important decisions. It may not be all night, although that could be a very healthy practice. Wouldn't it be great if every Christian were to devote an entire night to prayer, to seek the mind of God and the direction to go before getting married, accepting or quitting a job, starting a business, or filing for divorce? Imagine if all the decisions we made in life followed the pattern of Jesus Christ, who prayed before he decided anything important.

Recently Charleen and I had breakfast with a couple in Wisconsin, and in the course of our table conversation, he asked my advice about something. His response to my suggestion was "Before I could make a decision like that I would have to pray about it for two or three days." I liked that—it is a communion with God that shows dependence on the Lord rather than independence from the Lord.

Several years ago the members of Wooddale Church voted that I become senior pastor of the church. It was a major decision both for Wooddale and for my family and me. One of the most comforting and exciting parts of the call was the information that long before they ever heard my name, over four hundred Wooddalers had committed in writing to daily prayer that the right decision would be made. We who are Christians, who pattern our lives after Jesus Christ, would do well to so prepare for all the important decisions of our lives.

One more part of Jesus' biography helps us see his pattern for prayer. Matthew 26:36–44 is a part of the New Testament that I always read with difficulty, for it was a time of great pain and great sorrow in Jesus' life. It was the night before he was crucified, and no matter how many times I read it I always feel like I am snooping in a place too holy for me to look.

> Then Jesus went with his disciples to a place called Gethsemane, and he said to them, "Sit here while I go over there and pray." He took Peter and the two sons of Zebedee along with him, and he began to be sorrowful and troubled. Then he said to them, "My soul is overwhelmed with sorrow to the point of death. Stay here and keep watch with me."
>
> Going a little farther, he fell with his face to the ground and prayed, "My Father, if it is possible, may this cup be taken from me. Yet not as I will, but as you will."
>
> Then he returned to his disciples and found them sleeping. "Could you men not keep watch with me for one hour?" he asked Peter. "Watch and pray so that you will not fall into temptation. The spirit is willing, but the body is weak."
>
> He went away a second time and prayed, "My Father, if it is not possible for this cup to be taken away unless I drink it, may your will be done."
>
> When he came back, he again found them sleeping, because their eyes were heavy. So he left them and went away once more and prayed the third time, saying the same thing.

That night Jesus experienced deep sorrow because of the horrors in his life. He grieved over the losses he faced. He felt the pain of other people's sins. He felt the helplessness of the inevitable.

I think it sad that too often when we read this we get hung up on the sleepiness of his followers. That's really not what this is all about. It is a glimpse into the sorrow and submission of Jesus Christ. Jesus did what we all do—he tried to think of alternatives. He prayed, "My Father, if it is possible, may this cup be taken from me." When we're up against it, when we feel crushed in by things that may or may not be our fault, we plead with God, asking for alternatives.

Jesus was lying facedown on the ground praying with such intensity that he had to take a break, and he went to check on his friends. Then he went back and he prayed the same prayer again: "Father, there's got to be some other way. Wouldn't it be possible for me not to drink this terrible cup that you have put on the table before me?" He struggled through and then prayed the same thing. "God, there's got to be some way out of this. In all of your infinite wisdom there's got to be another approach. But not my will, but yours be done."

It was hard. It was the same prayer many of us pray, "God, there's got to be another way." But finally we submit and say, "God, if that's the cup you've laid before me, if that's what you want, I'll drink it. Not my will, but your will." You see, the issues of sorrow and submission are real, and they are the depth of communion with God.

So prayer defined is communion with God that is patterned after Jesus. When the followers of Jesus saw and heard him pray, they said, "This is special, this is different—that's the way *we* want to pray!" Luke 11:1 says:

> One day Jesus was praying in a certain place. When he finished, one of his disciples said to him, "Lord, teach us to pray."

I would like you to consider a challenge to pray that prayer, whatever it may mean: "Lord, teach me how to pray."

O Lord Jesus, for those of us who have prayed that prayer, please answer. Teach us to pray as you prayed; open heaven to make it a priority, in private as well as in public, for the big and small decisions of life—even to the depth of sorrow and submission.

Teach us to pray. Amen.

❧

Chapter Eight

Teach Us to Pray

If prayer is communion with God, important and powerful, why is it that people talk about prayer as if they are not very good at it? Often I hear people say, "I don't pray enough. It's a weak area of my life." I'm not sure I've ever heard anyone say, "When it comes to prayer, that is my greatest strength. I'm really good at praying. I'd say overall I'm in about the 99th percentile." I think the reason is that prayer, like a lot of things in life, is rather simple at the front end but it gets increasingly complex as we move further into it.

Jesus told his followers: "But when you pray, go into your room, close the door and pray to your Father, who is unseen. Then your Father, who sees what is done in secret, will reward you" (Matthew 6:6).

With those words Jesus taught what is the cornerstone of a significant prayer life in relationship with God—private prayer. Praying alone.

PRAY ALONE, PRAY TOGETHER

The elements are simple, although doing it can be hard. It starts with a place. Jesus said, "Go into your room." It could be any room. It could be a bedroom, an unused room in the house, maybe a corner of the basement where no one else wants to go, or it may be in your car at lunch hour in some distant part of the parking lot. It takes a place and it takes a time. Some people have chosen early in the morning. There are some morning-type people who don't even need to set an alarm. They get up before dawn and pray every day. There are other people who pray during lunch hour or coffee break, and for some it's those final moments before going to sleep at night. Try to make it the same time every day. Start by taking five minutes to worship God and to tell him how great he is, to say, "I love you," to confess sin, to experience forgiveness, to say thank-you, and to ask—to present requests to God. Let the time increase naturally until the five becomes ten and the ten becomes fifteen minutes every day. For some people it may even stretch beyond that to more like half an hour.

The hard part is to do it. We have a thousand different distractions. Life is busy and life is full. And prayer, to be candid, is not a natural activity. It's a supernatural undertaking, and it's not easy to do. Because it is connecting with and deploying the power of God, it is entering into spiritual warfare. Satanic forces work to keep us from private prayer. But I'm convinced that for those who do it, it is without doubt the most significant and life-changing pursuit that any Christian can follow.

But as essential as private prayer is, there is an extra effectiveness and power when we pray together. Again, it was Jesus who said, "If two of you on earth agree about anything you ask for, it will be done for you by my Father in heaven. For where two or three come together in my name, there am I with them" (Matthew 18:19–20).

Prayer is entering into spiritual warfare.

Jesus doesn't explain why prayer together differs from private prayer, he just states it. By the way, this is not talking about a gathering where someone stands up front and says, "Let's all bow our heads and silently pray." That is just a lot of people privately praying in the same place at the same time. What is described here is when two or three people get together to pray and they agree concerning the direction of their prayer before the prayers are spoken and perhaps again after they have prayed. I try to understand exactly what occurs when two or three people pray that is different from when a person prays alone. The difference is probably a mixture of the natural and the supernatural.

The natural reason that prayer together is so powerful is because of the expectation that two Christians should come to agreement before they ask. There's a different dynamic whenever we do something together that is empowering in a way that doesn't happen when we are alone. Praying together also balances our private idiosyncrasies. We are far more likely to ask inappropriate and unbiblical prayers alone than in cooperation with other believers.

A physician once remarked to me that different dynamics take place with different combinations of antibiotics, but occasionally a synergism happens between two antibiotics and they are able to accomplish far more together than either one could accomplish independently. There's something natural about the compounding and multiplying effect of our prayers when we pray together.

But also something supernatural happens when two or three pray together. Jesus Christ is present in a way in which he is not present when we pray alone. He is there in presence and power in a way that is impossible to experience when we pray by ourselves.

We must first understand that prayer is a relationship. In fact, everything about prayer is based upon relationship. If there is no relationship then we're just talking to ourselves. The relationship may be good or bad, it may be new or old, it may be close or distant, warm or cold, but there is no such thing as prayer without relationship.

Remember when Jesus' followers said, "Teach us to pray"? His example for them was "Our Father who art in heaven, hallowed be your name." He started immediately with the relationship with the Father in heaven. Later, when explaining to them how prayer works, Jesus told them that when they talk to the Father in heaven to be sure to mention his name. People have prayed ever since "in Jesus' name," because Jesus gives us access to God in a way we wouldn't otherwise have. It's all about a relationship.

Prayer is to relationship as swimming is to water. You can pretend that you swim; you can go through the motions on dry land, but it isn't real unless you're in the water. In the same way, prayer is not the real thing unless it's in a relationship with God. Relationship is what makes true communion with God possible.

FACETS OF PRAYER

Perhaps a harder thing to understand about prayer is that it is multifaceted—like the different facets on a diamond. There are a lot of different parts to it. Some people think that prayer is just asking, but that is only a part of what prayer is.

The Bible gives many examples of the facets of prayer. First Samuel 1:11–15 is the prayer of the infertile Hannah who so much wanted to have a child. She went to the temple and prayed. The record says that she poured out her soul to the Lord. She was so emotional, so passionate, that they tried to kick her out of the temple because they thought she was drunk.

Asking is only a part of what prayer is.

In Psalm 88:1–2, the psalmist cried out to God to listen. Did you ever have a relationship with someone, and while you were talking you wondered if that person was listening at all? The psalmist said:

> O Lord, the God who saves me,
> day and night I cry out before you.

May my prayer come before you;
turn your ear to my cry.

It is almost as if the psalmist is reaching up and grabbing God's shoulder and saying, "Turn this way, turn your head and hear my cry. Listen to me, God!"

In almost all relationships there are complaints, and that is a facet of prayer as well. The psalmist in Psalm 142:1–2 said:

I cry aloud to the Lord:
I lift up my voice to the Lord for mercy.
I pour out my complaints before him;
before him I tell my trouble.

Jeremiah, one of the greatest prophets of the Old Testament, also complained to God. He prayed:

O Lord, you deceived me, and I was deceived;
you overpowered me and prevailed.
I'm ridiculed all day long; everyone mocks me. (20:7)

He's saying, "God, you tricked me and you used all your power to do me in." He wasn't complaining about somebody else. He was complaining to God about God.

Then, of course, prayer includes asking. In Matthew 7:7–8 Jesus said,

Ask and it will be given to you; seek and you will find; knock and the door will be opened to you. For everyone who asks receives; he who seeks finds; and to him who knocks, the door will be opened.

The Bible has many "asking" prayers. Paul in his letter to the Philippians says,

Do not be anxious about anything, but in everything, by prayer and petition, with thanksgiving, present your requests to God. And the peace of God, which transcends all understanding, will guard your hearts and your minds in Christ Jesus. (Philippians 4:6–7)

Sometimes prayer is passionate:

During the days of Jesus' life on earth, he offered up prayers and petitions with loud cries and tears to the one who could save him from death. (Hebrews 5:7)

Sometimes prayers are silent. Romans 8 gives an example of a person who is praying and runs out of words and says, "God, I don't know what else to say—I'm stuck." It says that the Holy Spirit picks up and starts praying on our behalf. I've had that happen. I've had times when I was praying and I couldn't come up with the words. Not that I ended the communication with God, but I stopped saying words and asked that the Holy Spirit pick up and say whatever words I should be saying because I couldn't figure them out.

One of the best examples of a good relationship is when we can be silent. You've got to be a really good friend with someone to be comfortable enough to be able to ride along in a car for an hour or two in silence. Sometimes prayer to God takes place in silence.

This is like other relationships that we have: husbands and wives, parents and children, employers and employees, and best of friends. Sometimes there is passion, sometimes silence, sometimes praising, sometimes pleading, sometimes comforting, and sometimes complaining. Prayer communicates in all these—and more—ways, all within a relationship with God.

But all these facets of prayer assume something. They assume that the person who prays believes in God. Even if you forget all the references we have looked at in this chapter, there is one that you ought to remember. Hebrews 11:6 says,

Without faith it is impossible to please God, because anyone who comes to him must believe that he exists and that he rewards those who earnestly seek him.

Do you think God hears and answers the prayers of atheists? Of unbelievers? I think he does. We've all heard stories of people who are not believers, but because of some wartime or emergency room experience blurt out a prayer that, to that person's surprise as much as everyone else's, God answers. Maybe that's been your experience. Perhaps even before becoming a Christian you prayed a prayer that God clearly answered. Maybe that was one of the reasons why you became a Christian.

I think the difference is that God has not obligated himself to answer. Someone who does not have a relationship with God through Jesus Christ cannot go to God and say, "God, you have committed in advance that you will hear me and answer me." But God, at least occasionally, out of his goodness and generosity, hears and answers the desperate prayers of people with whom he has no relationship. It's different for those who have a relationship with God through Jesus Christ, because with that relationship God has obligated himself. He has committed in writing that he will hear and that he will answer.

Think of it this way. If a total stranger walks up to me and asks me to do him a favor, I may or may not do it, depending on what he asks. We have no relationship, and I feel no obligation to him. On the other hand, if my wife asks me to do her a favor my answer is "Yes—what do you want me to do?" Because of the marriage relationship, we have an obligation to each other.

BEGIN TO PRAY

Once we understand the basics of prayer and have a relationship with God, the next step is to begin praying. I think that many of us pray little because we just never get started. And many people don't get started because they are afraid they won't get it right. They're afraid that somehow they won't be articulate. I often hear people say that they could never pray out loud in front of other people because they are afraid they won't know what to say or they might say the wrong thing. In fact, a lot of people never pray privately for the same reasons. They sense that there's a prescribed way to pray, and if you don't get it perfect, then the prayer doesn't count and you might offend God.

Talk to parents whose child or children live out of town, and ask them, "What would you say is the right way for your son or daughter to call you on the phone?" They will give you a blank stare in return. They have no idea what you are talking about. Parents who love their children will tell you there is no "right way." They are glad to get the call day or night, at home or at work. Sons and daughters can phone home when they have nothing special to talk about or when they face life's biggest crises. It's okay to call Mom and Dad to tell a joke or to cry, to dial direct or call collect. There just isn't a "right way."

And so it is with God. You don't need to worry about getting prayer "right." God loves to hear from you—any time, any place, any topic. You can ask him for money, plead for comfort, or just talk about what happened at the office during the day. God has amazing tolerance. He understands. So don't ignore him. Don't treat him as if he's not there and miss out on the greatest relationship you'll ever have.

Chapter Nine

No Answer

You meet a man who is very much in love and convinced that he has found the woman whom he should marry. He loves her and feels that he can make her happy in a way that no one else possibly could. He writes out the proposal and memorizes it word for word. To seal the deal he prays diligently and enthusiastically in the name of Jesus Christ that she will say yes and that they will be married. The moment comes, he delivers the proposal, and she says no.

You talk to a woman who really the needs the job she has applied for. Her children are hungry, they need shoes, and there's no money left. The job is a perfect match. The hours are right. The pay is good. The benefits are particularly important. She's one of the finalists. There are six or eight people in the final cut and she's in for the last interview. As a committed Christian she prays before that interview, asking that God will prepare the way for her, that he will make it happen, that she'll get the job. And again the answer is no.

Anyone who has done very much praying knows what a divine "no" is all about. Some people become angry with God when he turns them down. They write him off, and sometimes vent that hostility in rage against God's name, against God's people, against God's church. Other people have a fatalistic attitude. They say, "Well, if that's the way it's going to be, then that's what I've got to accept." How we respond to the divine "no" may be one of our most life-shaping decisions. It may even determine whether we ever pray again.

Many, when they hear God say no, quote the words of Jesus in Matthew 21:22: "If you believe, you will receive whatever you ask for in prayer." They say, "I believe; I really believe. I have so much faith that I was astounded when God didn't do it. What other conclusion can I come to except that the Bible must be wrong or that God is a liar?"

Is it really that simple? Is it really that clear-cut? Is that the way we think and operate in other areas of our lives?

There are people who believe that God will give them absolutely anything they ask for just because they believe. It's not that Jesus' promise isn't true. But we need to understand it in the context of the rest of what the Bible has to say—call it the fine print. Recall, for example, that Jesus on the night before he was crucified asked that the crucifixion be canceled. Three times he prayed that, and every time the answer was no. The apostle Paul, who had been used by God to heal many people, was turned down repeatedly when he was sick and prayed for a cure. Peter, another author of the New Testament, in 1 Peter 3:7 tells men not to be inconsiderate and disrespectful to their wives or their prayers will be hindered. In the Old Testament, Daniel the prophet prayed and thought he got a no, but then an angel appeared to him and said that he was sent from God with the answer yes as soon as Daniel prayed, but it took him twenty-one days to deliver the message because of a demon that delayed him.

Now if Jesus, Paul, Peter, and Daniel got a temporary or a permanent no to their requests, we should not be surprised if God also answers no to some of our prayers. Consider the whole matter from God's point of view.

A HEAVENLY POINT OF VIEW

Surely near the top of the list is that God sometimes says no because many of the things for which we pray would actually ruin us if God granted them. We are prone to ask for a life of ease, and yet we admit that it's the hardships of life that make us strong. We tend to pray that there be no suffering, and yet the Bible clearly explains that if we are to have solidarity with Jesus Christ we need to at least in part experience some of his suffering. We tend to pray for a quick answer to whatever we seek. But God counts patience an important virtue for us to learn.

It is a concept that every parent understands. Every parent has to say no sometimes to a pleading child simply because what is asked is not in the best interest of that child. Your two-year-old comes to you and asks for matches, and you say no. Your eight-year-old seeks an un-limited supply of candy that will rot his teeth, and you say no. Or your seventeen-year-old asks, "Could I have your checkbook and credit cards for spring break?" In each case you say no, not because you don't love the child, not because you don't care, not because you don't understand the child's perspective, but because it's not in that child's best interest to have those things.

Well, God is a parent, and a very good parent. God is so committed to us as children that he is willing to say no even if it will trigger our anger against him. But that's not the only reason that God says no.

Common sense tells us that God can't say yes to two contradictory prayers. Soldiers on opposing sides, on the eve of a battle, pray for victory. Some people this morning prayed for rain and others prayed for sunshine. There are a dozen people who pray that they will get the same job that has been advertised in the newspaper. God will say yes to some and no to others. We need to understand that the God who created the laws of physics—including that two objects cannot occupy the same space at the same time because that would be contradictory—is the God who has created the law of noncontradiction. He does not contradict himself. I think there are millions, probably billions, of cases every day where God receives requests that contradict each other. And so to some he says yes and to some he says no.

Or it may be that God turns us down because what we ask for is inappropriate. There are those who have prayed, "God, help me to rob the bank today" or "Don't let the IRS figure out that I cheated." People make all kinds of inappropriate prayer requests.

At the end of Luke 9, there's a story of Jesus and his followers on their way to Jerusalem. The route that they took was through Samaria, where there was racial animosity between the Jews and the Samaritans. It was too late for them to get to Jerusalem that night, so the followers of Jesus asked if they could stay overnight in the Samaritan town. The Samaritans hated Jerusalem and they hated the Jews, so they said no. The followers of Jesus didn't particularly like the Samaritans either, so they had a simple and straightforward prayer request, to bring down fire from heaven and burn the village to cinders. It was an especially inappropriate prayer, because it was based on racial hatred. And the answer to the racist prayer was no. While we may think that they were terrible to pray that prayer, the truth is that, at least on occasion, we too pray inappropriate prayers: that she'll break her leg, that he'll lose his job, or that their company will not do particularly well. God says no because the prayer is inappropriate. And it's a good thing. We ought to be grateful that God says no to such prayers.

On other occasions God says no to a prayer because relationships are in need of repair. For example, I mentioned that Peter said a man's prayers may be hindered because he treats his wife disrespectfully or with a lack of consideration. Peter understood from experience that relationship is an important part of prayer. Not just with the wife or husband, but especially with God. For it is important to God that we have a right relationship with him. And so we ask God for something and he says, "Let's straighten our relationship out first, and after we've done that you can ask me again."

Sin messes up our relationship with God, so confession should precede asking for anything. The good news is that God promises that if we confess our sins he will forgive us our sins and cleanse us and restore a good relationship. It is important to God that our relationships be right.

Confession should precede asking for anything.

I wonder how many times good prayer requests are spoken and God has said, "Wait a minute, first you need to straighten things out with your son or your daughter." Or he says, "Look, you have been holding a grudge against your old boss ever since you left the company, and you've got to forgive her even if she doesn't deserve it. You need to straighten out that relationship and then come back and ask me again." Relationship is important to God.

Or it may be that God simply wills something that is different from what I will. Some say then, "What's the point of praying? If God's going to do what he wants anyway, why bother to pray?" A better question would be, "What's the point of having a God if he is always going to do whatever we want?" It's a good thing that God doesn't let my will rule over his will. God is wise, and it's a good thing that his will prevails in the choices that have to be made.

Another reason that God says no is simply because the time isn't right. The answer may not be "no," but "later." Now is not the right time. When you read the biography of Jesus, you see that whenever he does something spectacular like changing water to wine, making a blind person see, or a lame person walk, his followers say, "Let's tell everybody that you are the Christ."

And Jesus says, "No, not now. My time hasn't come."

Then they ask him six weeks later, "Can we tell everybody now? Can we announce to all of Israel that you are the King, the Son of David?"

"Not yet. Not now." It isn't that Jesus was rejecting what they were requesting; in fact, he intended what they requested. But it was a matter of timing.

And so it is with many of the things about which we talk to God. God is dealing with putting all of the pieces together for many lives, not just ours. He is pulling together many factors to bring them to the perfect timing. And so "no" may simply be "wait."

We often say, "His timing was just a little bit off," or "She was in the right place at the right time," or "Timing is everything." So what seems to be a no from God may simply be "Now is not the time."

Maybe it's simply because something else is more important. It isn't that what we ask for isn't good; it's that God has something more important that needs to be accomplished. It may be that we're asking him so that we'll look good, but it's more important that he look good. It may be that he has an idea that we've never dreamed of.

When I was in my twenties, I applied for a doctoral program at an Ivy League university, and I really had my heart set on it. I went for the interview with the head of the department, and he said to me, "You match all the qualifications for this program, but so do all the other seven hundred applicants, and we have only twelve slots open for next year." I still prayed confidently that God would get me what I wanted, and that was admission to that school. The answer was no. I ended up applying to another school and went there instead.

Maybe God has an idea that we've never dreamed of.

God was good to me in saying no. I learned from professors, made friends, and benefited in ways that would have been impossible had

God answered my prayer the way I wanted. In retrospect, I see that I was most interested in getting a degree from an Ivy League university, and God was most interested in getting me the education I needed.

Sometimes we ask the right thing, but we do it for the wrong reason. Let's suppose that I pray that you will come to Wooddale Church, because here you will experience the Bible teaching and the Christian nurture that will shape your life wonderfully and positively. But my real motive for the prayer, never spoken either to you or to God, is that I need to borrow some money, and you look like an easy touch. I have no intention of paying that money back. I figure that if you come to church here, then you and I can get acquainted, and I can ask you for the cash that I seek. God says no to my prayer to protect you from me. Instead he sends you to some other fine church and there you grow spiritually, and there you are nurtured, and there you become all that God wants you to become.

It wasn't that my prayer was bad—my prayer was good. But the motive behind the prayer was something completely different from what that prayer appeared to be. I think if we're honest about it we'll admit that we ask God for a lot of things with bad motivations. God would teach us some very bad habits if he gave us everything we wanted for the wrong reasons. He loves us far too much to do that.

We've considered eight reasons that God may have for saying no to prayers, which is by no means a complete list, but now let's make it a little more personal and talk about how to respond when God says no to our heartfelt requests.

What to Do When God Says No

What if I plead my heart out to God, and I have no place else to turn, and the answer is still no? What do I do? How do I respond? I'd say that a place to begin is to seek an explanation from God. Ask him to explain which of these eight reasons, or some other reason not on the list, applies. Is it not for now, or is there something wrong with my relationship, or is my motive out of place? Remember that God is a loving God, he's generous, he delights in giving good and perfect gifts to all those who are his. Most often he will tell us why he says no and help us to understand. He wants us to know. But if he doesn't explain why, then that's God choice to make.

If we're parents, we've been there. I remember times when our children were young and they would ask for a bike or a toy or to go someplace special, and we'd say, "No, we can't do that." They would ask again and again, and finally I would use the ultimate weapon of all parents: "Look, I'm the father, you're the kid, and the answer is no!" That never convinces a child, but it's something that parents have to say; it's part of the routine of parenthood. Perhaps the reason we don't want to explain to them is that the bike has already been bought for a Christmas present or that we're planning a trip to the amusement park as a surprise. Sometimes parents say no for very good reasons that just can't be explained.

Whether God explains or not, the next thing to do is to submit to God's decision. When my heart pleads for something and the answer is no, it is not an easy thing to submit to what God says. But when we refuse to submit, we are trying to become God. It's almost as if I'm saying, "God, I know better than you know. My choices are better than your choices. I'm smarter than you are." That's a dangerous thing to do with God.

And so I submit to him. I tell him that I trust him. We trust Jesus to save us from sin and hell. We trust God to give us eternal life. If we can trust him for the big things like eternity, heaven and hell, life and death, surely we should trust his ability to decide how to best answer our prayers. Trusting is what being a Christian is all about.

If we have asked him to explain and we have said that we will submit, what then? If God still says no, I'd say to ask again. Repeat the request.

The Bible is full of examples that encourage us to keep coming back and asking over and over. That's what Paul did, and that's what Jesus did. That's what the Bible says we are to do.

Surely we should trust God's ability to decide how to best answer our prayers.

For years my daily prayer list has followed the same format, even though some of the names and requests change. For more years than I can remember, there is one particular request for which the answer has been no. It's obviously very important to me or I would not have repeated it so many thousands of times. I've asked God to explain to me why. I have chosen to submit, and it's not been easy to submit to what his choice might be. And I have concluded that it is a prayer that I am to keep praying, even if the yes that I request doesn't come for years. We just need to be sure that when we repeat requests, we have first asked God to explain and we have made sure that we submit.

Think of some pressing and important prayer to which God has answered no. With that specific prayer in mind, I invite you to pray to God:

Lord, help me to understand why you say no, even if it will be a difficult lesson for me to learn. Grant me the patience in waiting to understand. And God, I submit to you and will accept your answer with gratitude and faith, even if I never understand why—because I trust you. Amen.

CHAPTER TEN

RESPONSE TO A MESSAGE

Our human imagination can run wild when trying to picture angels, assuming them to have wings and flowing white robes and almost invariably playing harps.

It really doesn't make a lot of difference how we imagine angels, for it is not their physical appearance that defines what they are. The word *angel* means messenger, so they are the mail carriers, the message carriers of God. They are the ones who on some rare occasions have appeared to human beings. In virtually every description of those appearances, they are described as being like men, having ordinary appearance much like us.

Angels may look like men, but they are very different. They are a totally different order of God's creation. They are more powerful, more intelligent, and they have immortality. They are as different from us as we are from ants. We are bigger, better, and more intelligent than ants, and in the same way, angels are bigger, better, and more intelligent than we are.

The Bible tells very little about angels. We are told that by human methods of counting, they are innumerable, although God does keep track of them. He has a ranking system, and he has every one of them named.

One of those angels who appeared to human beings God named Gabriel, which means in Hebrew *God is powerful.* He appears only twice in the Bible, and if we may guess from the absence of other information, we may surmise that he spends most of eternity simply waiting for a task to be done. For thousands of years at a time Gabriel stands at the side of the throne of God and simply waits. But when he is given an assignment, it is an extraordinarily important assignment.

Extraordinary Assignments

By biblical record it was in the sixth century B.C. that Gabriel appeared to a Hebrew man named Daniel. Daniel had been carried away into captivity by an invading nation, was first treated as a slave, but eventually became one of the highest-ranking officials, and some say second only to the emperor himself in power. An Old Testament book is named after him.

Gabriel appeared to Daniel in order to give him an overview of future history and to tell him precisely what was going to happen. When Daniel saw and heard Gabriel, he was dumb struck and fell flat on his face in fear. After Gabriel spoke and left, Daniel was sick and trembling for days. He was astounded for years afterward as he reflected on that experience. While I am sure Gabriel put God's message in the lowest common denominator of human language, it still was extremely difficult for Daniel to understand. When we read Gabriel's words in Daniel 8 we, too, find it hard to understand because our terminology and our way of thinking is so different from that of heaven.

When the message was told, Gabriel returned to heaven and stood again by the throne of God and waited five hundred years before God gave him another assignment in the record of biblical history. But when he was given his second assignment, it was by far the most important that he had ever been given, that any angel had ever been given, that anyone had ever been given. Gabriel was to go to a Jewish peasant girl and announce to her that God would enter human life and flesh within her body. It was something that I think Gabriel himself could not fully comprehend.

Gabriel had the equally formidable task of taking that which God had communicated to him as an angel and somehow translating it into words that a teenage Jewish girl would understand. I can only guess at what angels feel and think. I know that they are preachers far superior to me, and I probably attribute to them more human characteristics than they rightly deserve. Do you think angels prepare? Here was a message that had to be declared not only to Mary but also to all of humankind for all of history to follow. There could not be a stammer or a stutter. There could not be an imprecise or ill-chosen word. It had to be done in an absolutely correct way.

Then the time came. This was one assignment for which God would tolerate no delay. He had planned it for all of eternity, and it was to be done precisely when and where God said it was to be done. The angel Gabriel stepped out of the glories of heaven to a small city called Nazareth in the region of Galilee in Northern Palestine. He came and assumed a human disguise. We know this because Mary was gripped not by his appearance, but by his words. Not by the way he looked, but by the way he spoke and by what he said. Those words were prophetic. That is, they were words of that which was to come, a telling of the future before it happened. Gabriel was as much a prophet in the announcement that he gave as were Isaiah and Micah centuries before.

The angel Gabriel stepped out of the glories of heaven to a small city called Nazareth.

The difference was that his prophecy would come true not in hundreds of years but in hundreds of days.

We have the record of that Christmas conversation that took place between the angel Gabriel and the Virgin Mary in Luke 1. It is divided into three monologues. The first part says,

> In the sixth month, God sent the angel Gabriel to Nazareth, a town in Galilee, to a virgin pledged to be married to a man named Joseph, a descendent of David. The virgin's name was Mary. The angel went to her and said, "Greetings, you who are highly favored! The Lord is with you."
>
> Mary was greatly troubled at his words and wondered what kind of greeting this might be. (Luke 1:26–29)

In the Latin Bible, the word *greetings* is rendered *ave* from which we get the expression "Ave Maria." But Mary, of course, didn't speak nor understand Latin or even the Greek in which the New Testament first was written. Her native tongue was Aramaic.

The words he spoke were exactly right. She was highly favored. God had chosen Mary, not only as the woman from all of her generation but also as the woman of his choice from all of human history. He especially chose her to be the mother of his Son, chose her to give her genetic imprint to God in human form. Think of that! It was the genetic makeup of Mary that determined how tall he would be, the color of his eyes and hair, and the expressions on his face. And not just as a baby in a manger in a cave in Bethlehem, but through adolescence and into adulthood. It was the genetic appearance of Mary that Jesus the Son of God has even today, for the incarnation was not undone when the last word of the Gospel was written. Jesus was fully God's Son and still is, but it is also true that he was fully Mary's son and still is. Indeed, she was highly favored and God was with her. She was a very special young woman.

Now while Gabriel's words were right, he certainly didn't set Mary at ease. This stranger with his unusual greeting astounded her. Whether Gabriel liked it or not, Mary was scared—scared and troubled. She was upset because she had no categories into which she could plug the words that had been spoken. There was no shelf in the library of her mind where they fit.

I find in her a striking humility. I believe that she was genuinely surprised. She never dreamed that this would be her calling in life. She never imagined that she was any better or any different from any other girl of her generation. In fact, if I correctly read between the lines, she imagined that there were others who were far more qualified than she. Perhaps it is that simplicity of humility that at least, in part, caused God to choose her. She said nothing. When Gabriel greeted her and said she was highly favored and God was with her, she was silent; she didn't know what to say. She didn't know what to think. It was unthinkable to her.

Sensing her fear and her silence, he spoke again. The second part of his message is in Luke 1:30–34. This time he began by saying, "Do not be afraid, Mary, for you have found favor with God."

Have you ever discovered that words alone don't chase away fear? When you are traumatized, scared speechless, when you think that this is the worst moment of your life, or you fear that it is the prelude to far worse things to come, and someone says, "Don't be afraid—it's okay. Everything is going to work out fine"—don't you find that those words can be superficial and hollow? That sometimes it would almost be better if they were not said?

> "Do not be afraid, Mary."

But Gabriel wasn't speaking his own words, for he was an angel, a messenger of God. These were God's words that Gabriel spoke; and God's words, unlike our words, can never be counted as hollow sounds and syllables, for each word of God always comes with the power of

God. When Gabriel spoke the words to Mary, "Do not be afraid," they brought with them the calming power of God himself.

You may wonder, did Mary understand that? Did she feel that power, and was she comforted and changed? Yes, in part she was. But the words were to linger in her ears, be repeated on her lips, and echo in her mind for the rest of her life. "Do not be afraid, Mary, you have found favor with God."

With her heart at least somewhat calmed, Gabriel continued the essential message that he had come to deliver.

> You will be with child and give birth to a son, and you are to give him the name Jesus. He will be great and will be called the Son of the Most High. The Lord God will give him the throne of his father David, and he will reign over the house of Jacob forever; his kingdom will never end. (Luke 1:31–32)

Gabriel had given the message that he had come to give and it was finished. She would become pregnant, and she was to name the baby Jesus. He would be great, the Messiah, the Son of the Most High, a king who would rule over Israel on David's throne, but more than that, a king who would rule over a kingdom that would last forever and ever.

A simple peasant girl in the little city of Nazareth, she answered Gabriel with a disarming question that I suspect he never anticipated. She said, "How will this be since I'm a virgin?" Gabriel had just given her the biggest news in all of celestial history. He had told her something that no other human being knew. She and she alone had that information, the great love act of God, the most profound theological truth ever revealed, and she said, "I'm a virgin, how am I going to have a baby?"

The answer comes in verses 35 to 38. While it is true that Gabriel had been sent to make this supernatural announcement, when it came to the actual conception, God would never delegate that to any angel. It was something that God would do himself. God had chosen to draw a supernatural veil around Mary that no one could see. His Holy Spirit performed a miracle in her body that nobody else would ever fully understand. For two thousand years people have been trying to explain it and figure it out, but no one has been able to penetrate that veil. No one has been able to understand the extraordinary miracle to the point that they could answer Mary's question, "How?" God would do it and God would never explain it.

Gabriel did the best he could. He gave his answer like this, "Mary, the Holy Spirit will come upon you, and the power of the Most High will overshadow you. So the holy one to be born will be called the Son of God." I suspect that Gabriel's answer caused more questions in Mary's mind than she had before. Surely she wondered, *When is this going to happen? Today, or are you talking about something that's ten years off? And where? Is it going to happen here in Nazareth, or someplace else? What will it be like when the Holy Spirit does this to me? Will I feel it? Will I know when it's happening? Will I be scared?*

Showing special sensitivity to Mary's dilemma, Gabriel added something to his announcement that may seem somewhat disconnected: "Even Elizabeth your relative is going to have a child in her old age, and she who was said to be barren is in her sixth month." You see, that was something Mary could understand. She had this older relative named Elizabeth. Everybody knew that Elizabeth was infertile, and that was not a compliment for a woman in ancient Israel. She was far past the normal childbearing age. Yet Gabriel said that Elizabeth was pregnant, in fact six months pregnant.

As astounding as it was, it was something that Mary could verify. It was in a sense the gift of a lesser miracle to prime Mary's pump of faith so that she could begin to understand a far greater miracle. Gabriel added this word to explain to her that she was dealing with God, and with God nothing is impossible.

Mary's mind must have been spinning and her heart must have been pounding. How could she in two minutes comprehend that which theologians in two millennia have not yet been able to adequately explain?

CHARACTER COUNTS

What Mary said next is more a measure of her godliness and character than anything else. I want to be careful that we don't underestimate this woman. For while it is true that she was young and while it is true that she was poor and lived in a time and place where women had low priority and poor education in society, understand that she was the one whom God had chosen to mother his Son. She was not ignorant or stupid, and yet when she faced this crisis, it wasn't her intelligence or her education that came through, it was her character. As is so often the case with all of us, when we face the traumas, the difficulties, and the opportunities of life, it is more often our character than our intelligence that prescribes what will be our response.

It was a reflection of her character when she said, "I am the Lord's servant. May it be to me as you have said." No, she did not understand, but she accepted it because it was from God. She accepted it because she was God's servant, and that's what servants do with their masters; they accept what they say. She accepted it because she knew God to be trustworthy.

She knew God to be trustworthy.
❧

I think we can learn from Mary's lessons. I think we can practice Mary's character. For we, too, face our surprises, our traumas, our difficulties, our opportunities in life. They may be different, but every one of us has things in our lives that we don't understand. There is a woman who is pregnant, but doesn't want to have a baby. There is another woman who desperately wants to have a baby, but can't become pregnant. There's the family that's being transferred that wants to stay where they are; there's a family that wants to move, but can't get the transfer. There's health and cancer, joy and sorrow, and life and death. We have long lists of all the circumstances that pile into our lives, that catch us by surprise, that leave us dumb struck so we don't know what words to speak, until finally we blurt out to God, "How can this be? How can this be happening?" Sometimes God in his grace gives us at least a partial answer, sometimes not. But even after we have gotten that partial answer, we don't fully understand. We can't fit all the pieces together. It doesn't mesh with our dreams. It doesn't quite fit the plan.

It is in the midst of those circumstances of life that we have the opportunity in our character to follow Mary—to accept because he is God, to accept because we are his servants, to accept because he is trustworthy. Luke adds an explanation. When the Christmas conversation is over, he says, "Then the angel left her." As far as I know, Gabriel hasn't been back since. So for two thousand years, he has stood by the throne of God waiting for another assignment, waiting for God to again send him out to do something special.

As far as Mary is concerned, and as far as the record tells, these are the only words that she ever got from him, but Gabriel and God counted them to be enough to get her through her pregnancy, enough to get her through the difficult birth under the less-than-best circumstances in Bethlehem. They were enough for Jesus' childhood, his adolescence, and his grown-up years. These words were enough for when he was crucified and she watched him die, and enough for the rest of her life.

Enough for her and enough for us—the same words. "Don't be afraid! Call him Jesus. He will be the son of the Most High God and his kingdom reign will last forever."

CHAPTER ELEVEN

WORTHY OF HIS CALL

The early settlers of our country had an interesting way of getting even with those they didn't like. Out on Cape Cod and the offshore islands of Nantucket and Martha's Vineyard, even after hundreds of years most of the tombstones are easily read in terms of name and dates and epitaph. Sometimes in just a few words you can learn a great deal about the person's life. Normally the tombstones were placed with the inscription facing the leeward side of the Cape so that the lettering was protected from the wear and tear of salty winds and abrasive sand. But if the deceased was disliked, his tombstone was set toward the windward side of the Cape. In only a few years his name, dates, and epitaph were completely erased. I have often walked those colonial cemeteries and wondered about those whose gravestones are smooth and letterless. It's almost as if they never lived, as if they counted for nothing.

It's a frightening thing to count for nothing, to be gone but never missed, to have lived life and left no mark, as if one had never been. Most of us spend much of our lives trying to leave some kind of a memory, some kind of a mark—to make our lives count. We work hard, have children, write books, build monuments, or climb mountains—anything to leave our mark.

In A.D. 51 the apostle Paul prayed a prayer for his boastworthy Thessalonian friends. It is a good prayer for all of us who want our lives to count.

> With this in mind, we constantly pray for you, that our God may count you worthy of his calling, and that by his power he may fulfill every good purpose of yours and every act prompted by your faith. We pray this so that the name of our Lord Jesus may be glorified in you, and you in him, according to the grace of our God and the Lord Jesus Christ. (2 Thessalonians 1:11–12)

A CALL FROM GOD

Paul prays that God will "count you worthy of his calling." There's a complicated concept that's rooted here; a concept that is well worth learning. The concept begins with a call. The call comes from God and it is the call to salvation. God calls individuals to repent of sin, to receive Jesus Christ as Savior, and to acknowledge him as Lord so they can live for him now and be with him for eternity.

As impressive as it is to get a call from the president of the United States, it's nothing compared to a call from God. And God is a most effective caller! He first decides whom to call, and then he makes the call and follows it up all the way to heaven. It's described in Romans 8:30 like this: "And those he predestined, he also called; those he called, he also justified; those he justified, he also glorified."

Just because someone gets a call does not mean that person deserves a call. In fact, the Bible is quite plain in saying that no one deserves a call from God to salvation. Every call God makes is totally out of the goodness of his heart. It's just because he chooses to. It's just because he's generous and gracious. We never have a right to say, "God should call me." Absolutely no one is worthy of God's list.

Look at the powerful and important truth here. The reason anyone is worthy of his call is solely because God counts us as worthy— not because we are worthy in and of ourselves. "With this in mind, we constantly pray for you, that our God may count you worthy of his calling."

Visualize two pieces of paper. One of them is a $100 bill and the other one is a $1 bill. Now, which is worth more? Most people would rightly say it is the $100 bill. Actually they're worth about the same in terms of paper and ink, a few cents at most. Ah, you say, but this one is worth a hundred times more than that one. Why is that so? Because our government counts this one to be worth a hundred times more, not because the paper or ink has any greater value. The difference in value is in the way it is counted.

We're pretty near worthless in and of ourselves.

And so it is with us. The reason we have infinite value is not because of who we are but because of the way God counts us. The truth is that we're pretty near worthless in and of ourselves. But God counts us as worthy of his Son's death, as worthy of salvation. He counts us as worthy of his call and worthy of his heaven. It's an extraordinary thing.

Paul is saying that if we're going to be $100 bills then we should act like $100 bills. If we're going to be Christians then we should act like Christians. But sometimes we get confused about what we're worth. God counts us as worth a hundred bucks. He counts us as very valuable, but often we spend our lives as if we were worth one dollar.

EVERY GOOD PURPOSE

The point of the rest of verse 11 is that we act what we're worth. It's the prayer that God will make good dreams come true. Paul writes, "That by his power he may fulfill every good purpose of yours, and every act prompted by your faith." Every good purpose. Every good act. Every good dream.

Everybody dreams. Sometimes we remember our dreams, but most of the time we forget. The ones we remember can be divided into the categories of good or bad. We wake up from some dreams in delight, feeling great. Then there are those dreams from which we wake up frightened or panic-stricken.

Dreams and purpose are somewhat similar—not quite synonymous, but close. Purpose is a sense of what we want to do and where we want to go; how we want to act out the resources that we have in the time that is ours. Some people have good purposes and some people have bad purposes. Even Christians counted worthy have both. We are torn between parallel dreams. On the one hand there is a dream to do good, to live right; but at the same time there is a dream to do evil and to live wrong. When we have competing dreams there's a pull for us to be self-centered and a pull to be Christ-centered. There's a competition in our lives over which dream will somehow be turned into reality.

Life's dreams and life's purposes are serious business, and at some point we have to decide what we're going to do with life. Which of those competing dreams are we going to seek to make come true? Which will be the triumphant purpose for which we shall live?

It seems like an easy choice. It seems as if you obviously choose the good over the bad. If you are a Christian, you choose to be Christ-centered rather than self-centered. We seek to be constructive rather than destructive. But it isn't that simple. When we choose the good, it may be painful to leave behind the bad. Sometimes the temptation to that which is negative is extraordinary. Sometimes we become addicted to that which we ought not to do. And so there is a price to be paid to choose the good dream. There is a price that comes with the right purpose.

Paul is praying for his Thessalonian friends and all followers of Jesus Christ that we will have God's power to make the good dreams and purposes happen and to make the bad purposes disappear. We've got to decide. Could we appropriate the power of God in such a way in our lives that the choice is clearly made, that we'll do what is right and good, that our dreams will conform with God's dreams and our purposes will become his purposes?

But it's more than dreams being prayed about here. It's more than purposes. It's more than something we sketch out on a piece of paper as the plan for our lives. It's something that has to be turned into action. Paul adds to his prayer that this power of God be used to "fulfill . . . every act prompted by your faith," assuming that we have faith in God and that faith is the instrument for doing what is right. It's not just purposing good. It's not just dreaming right. It's doing something about it.

> *If we are really counted worthy by God through Jesus Christ, then let's behave that way.*

Let's make it simple. If we are really $100 bills, not $1 bills, let's act like it. If we are really counted worthy by God through Jesus Christ, then let's behave that way. Are we profane? Let's clean up our speech. Are we thieves? Let's quit stealing. Are we immoral in our intent and our relationships? Let's revise our intent. Are we going the wrong direction in life? Let's pay the price and go the right direction. Let's get serious about breaking sinful habits and seek that which is moral, good, and true. Let's behave in a way consistent with the faith that we have in the God who has counted us worthy of heaven through Jesus Christ.

A simple example comes from author Jamie Buckingham. He tells about going to a restaurant with a friend and how that friend was demanding and unkind, even demeaning, to the waitress. Buckingham explains he was somewhat embarrassed when, after treating the waitress in that fashion, his friend insisted when the meal arrived that they pray audibly together. At the end of the meal when the check came, he left no tip. Buckingham said that later he managed to slip back into the restaurant and found the waitress. He gave her a double tip and said, "I'm doing this for two reasons: to pay you for putting up with my friend and to give you a blessing from God." She cried at his generosity and sensitivity.

He went on to talk about conversations with numerous waitresses who said very candidly that they would much rather have a boisterous party of half-drunk unbelievers than a group of quieter but demanding churchgoers—because church people didn't tip much, if they tip at all.[1]

That anecdote may be irrelevant to you. You probably are a twenty-five percent tipper! But it's simply saying that we as Christians are to behave in a way that is consistent with the worth that God has counted for us. Let's live morally; speak kindly; behave generously; set a Christ-like example in our behavior for all in earth and heaven to see, but not for ourselves—for Jesus.

In 2 Thessalonians 1:12, Paul writes, "We pray this so that the name of our Lord Jesus Christ may be glorified in you, and you in him, according to the grace of our God and the Lord Jesus Christ."

God both gets and gives glory. To glorify means to enhance the reputation of Jesus' name. I get a little uncomfortable sometimes when I hear myself and other people pray and speak about the name of Jesus Christ, using the word *name* pretty much the way we use names in our society. Names meant something different when the Bible was written. We use names as a means of identification. However, in biblical times a name meant more than a mark of identification. It represented the

---

[1] Jamie Buckingham, in *Charisma* magazine, n.d.

personality and character of the person. This verse is saying that we are to live lives in a way that enhances the reputation of Jesus Christ.

Names are still important and the reputation that goes with a name is important. Companies try to identify their names with quality through slogans: "The quality goes in before the name goes on," for example, or claiming that every product is signed by the artisan who made it. Putting your name on something means you're willing to stand behind it.

Do you know why the dollar is considered to be one of the hard currencies of the world? Did you know that all oil trading in the world is done in dollars? And did you know that many currencies of the world aren't worth a thing outside of their own country? They're like the paper currency in a Monopoly game. It might be worth something in the game, but it's not worth much anywhere else.

While traveling with my wife and daughter in Eastern Europe we were astounded to deal with people who refused to take their own currency, insisting that we pay them in U.S. dollars—even U.S. coins. In most countries people don't want foreign coins. But we found that in some of these countries they insisted on our coins, rather than their coins. That's because they recognize the tremendous value of the U.S. dollar as a hard currency. Do you know what makes the difference? It's not the piece of paper or the ink; it's because of the name written across the face of it: The United States of America.

As Christians, the name on our label is Jesus Christ.

The name makes a difference! The name assigns value. As Christians, the name on our label is Jesus Christ. Paul is praying that we will enhance the name of Jesus Christ; that we will behave in a way that is consistent with the one who gives us the value that we would not otherwise have. The wonderful part of it is that we have our reputation enhanced in the process. We reflect the glory of

Jesus Christ. "Jesus Christ is glorified in you, and you in him."

I once made my living driving a truck for a company that was owned by one man. Every truck in the entire fleet was painted white and had the owner's name and picture on both sides. He was concerned that we drive appropriately and not get tickets. He didn't like it when we cut people off, parked so it would inconvenience anyone, or did anything that would in any way bring disrepute to his company or to his name.

The comparison here is obvious. We wear the name and the face of Jesus Christ. Everywhere we go, every place we park, everyone we help, or everyone we cut off reflects not only upon us, but even more upon Jesus, because we wear his name and face.

What are you, a $1 bill or a $100 bill? I realize it's a poor analogy. Because if we're going to be consistent with the concept taught here, we are counted as invaluable by God. *Invaluable.* You and I are worth a fortune because he says we're worth a fortune—and he is God.

So let's live like it! Let's live like $1 million bills that have the name and face of Jesus Christ imprinted all over us. May we live the way we have been counted, for the glory of Jesus Christ.

❀

PHARISEE AND PUBLICAN

It was a wintry February day in London when my wife, Charleen, and I visited historic Westminster Abbey. We had not come to worship but rather to see the famous cathedral and especially to visit the tomb of David Livingstone located in the center of the main aisle of the nave.

My attention was particularly drawn that day to two different people. One was a well-dressed and seemingly sophisticated man who came in near the back of the Abbey and sat down. Then he flipped down the kneeling bench in front of him and knelt. I could tell by the movement of his lips and the intensity of his expression that he was praying. A short time later a disheveled woman came in whose ragged clothes made her look as if she had stepped out of the pages of *Oliver Twist*.

Trying to be as inconspicuous as I could, I stood over to the side and watched them both as they silently prayed. I was intrigued by the intensity with which they addressed God. I could not hear their prayers any better than I can hear yours or any other prayers that are uttered in silence. But those prayers that neither you nor I can hear are heard and understood by God.

And that's what Jesus is talking about in Luke 18:9–14:

> He also told this parable to some who trusted in themselves that they were righteous and despised others: "Two men went up into the temple to pray, one a Pharisee and the other a tax collector. The Pharisee stood and prayed thus with himself, 'God, I thank thee that I am not like other men, extortioners, unjust, adulterers, or even like this tax collector. I fast twice a week, I give tithes of all that I get.' But the tax collector, standing far off, would not even lift up his eyes to heaven, but beat his breast, saying, 'God, be merciful to me a sinner.' I tell you, this man went down to his house justified rather than the other; for everyone who exalts himself will be humbled, but he who humbles himself will be exalted" (RSV).

The simple message of the parable and the surrounding story is the message that God judges the proud and justifies the humble. With marvelous teaching skill Jesus communicates this message by telling a story using two men as examples.

TOO GOOD TO BE TRUE

One was a Pharisee and the other a publican. A Pharisee was an extraordinarily religious man in first-century Palestine who belonged to a very strict sect of Judaism. Pharisees were well known for their legalism. They carefully observed a long list of rules that dealt with almost every area of daily life. Others perceived them to be righteous, law-abiding Jews—quite a contrast to the publican who was a tax collector. However, we must understand that a tax collector then was not quite the same as a tax collector in our time and culture. A publican was an agent of the Roman forces who exacted taxes from his fellow Jews. Jews hated publicans because they were the ones who enabled the financing of the Roman occupation of their homeland. If you positioned these two men on a social ladder of Judaism, you would have the Pharisee somewhere near the top and the publican at the bottom.

This Pharisee was simply too good to be true. He knew his accomplishments and he was proud of them. It's an interesting expression of pride, because he believed in himself. He wasn't trying to deceive anyone. He really believed that he was better than anyone else and he thanked God for it.

The Pharisee had a double basis for his sense of goodness. The first was his comparison to others. He looked around and saw those who were extortioners, those who were unjust in their dealings with others, those who were adulterers, and he even saw a publican, and he knew that he was better than all of them. When he looked at his own life he knew that he did not take money from people by coercion, so he was not an extortioner. He knew that he was not unjust for he had meticulously kept the laws of Phariseeism. He'd never been to bed with anyone other than his wife so did not consider himself to be an adulterer, and he certainly was not taking money from his fellow Jews to fund the Roman occupation. So compared to everyone else the conclusion seemed obvious to him—he was better than all those around him. But that was not the only basis for his self-appraisal of goodness. He also was proud of his extraordinary religious behavior.

In those days Pharisees were known to fast twice a week, although the Old Testament law required only one fast in all the 365 days of the year—the Day of Atonement. Pharisees chose to fast every Monday and every Thursday. Those days are of particular interest because those were the market days in Jerusalem. If there were any days of the seven when someone fasting would stand out either by appearance or behavior it was surely those days. But it was not just a matter of what he didn't do, it was also a matter of what he did do. He had chosen to tithe everything, even though the Old Testament law only required that he give a tithe (or ten percent) of farming produce. This man was the type of individual who kept meticulous track of all sources of income and tithed on everything. He's the kind of person who if he got twenty dollars from his mother for his birthday would give two dollars extra the next time he came to the temple.

I sense very little hypocrisy in this man. He really believed that he was better than others. And, he was also a man of prayer. So we must not write him off as someone who was religiously insensitive. We also have to carefully analyze the words that he spoke. He expressed gratitude to God for the way he was and for all that he had. I suppose if there had been a Gallup poll in Jerusalem that year, most people would have agreed with the Pharisee's self-assessment. He would have gotten one of the highest ratings on the "goodness scale."

But he was too good to be true. His goodness may have been evident to him and to those who saw him, but not to God. All of this supposed goodness did not impress God in the least.

In fact, this Pharisee wasn't even praying to God. Verse 11 tells us that "the Pharisee stood and prayed thus with himself." I cannot think of a harsher indictment upon religious persons than to say, "When you pray in all your fervency, the only one who hears is you." This Pharisee was not righteous at all, because he was measuring by the wrong standard.

God does not measure righteousness by comparing us to other people, but measures righteousness by comparing us to himself. He does not rate us on what we have done, but on what he has done for us. The result is eternally different.

God measures righteousness by comparing us to himself.

William Barclay wrote of a trip he took from his native Scotland down into England by train. As the train passed through the Yorkshire moors he was impressed by a little whitewashed country cottage "which seemed to shine with an almost radiant whiteness." He did his business in England, and several days later took the return trip by train back to

Scotland. In the meantime there had been a heavy snowfall through Yorkshire. The moors that had been brown and green had been turned white by heavy snow. He looked out the window again and saw that same cottage, but this time he wrote, "Its whiteness seemed drab and soiled and almost gray in comparison with the virgin whiteness of the driven snow."[1]

You see, it all depends upon that to which we compare something. This Pharisee thought he looked great because he compared himself to extortioners, the unjust, adulterers, and tax collectors. But God's truth was that he looked pathetic compared to the righteousness of God.

What a sobering reality. Do we not also compare ourselves primarily to those with whom we compare favorably? Even as Christians do we not look at other people and say, "They read the wrong books, but I read the right books. They pray, but I pray better. They may go to church, but I go to a better church"? We make the comparison to make ourselves come out as good as we can be.

In different dress and with different titles, Pharisees abound in every generation. Today's Pharisees pray, "God, I thank you that I'm not like other people who take drugs, have AIDS, commit adultery, or abuse alcohol. God, I thank you that I have not delved into heresy and false teachings that are not consistent with your Word. I thank you, Father, that I'm not unjust as I see other people are in their businesses. I thank you that I'm an honest person and I do not do the things that other people do morally or ethically or in business or in religion. I thank you, Lord, that I'm faithful in my church attendance and that I scrupulously read the Bible and faithfully pray. I thank you, God, that I am able to write my check each week to you and to be one of your finest supporters."

In fact, modern Pharisees are seldom hypocrites. For when we say such things, I think we believe them. We are proud of who we are and

---

[1]William Barclay, *The Gospel of Luke* (Philadelphia: The Westminster Press, 1975), 225.

what we are not. We are grateful that we are not like the others.

Pharisees are blinded by their pride, and so deafened by their own perspective that they cannot hear their own words. I think there is some Pharisee in most of us! We're just not tuned in to it.

We have disdain for people who do not measure up to the standards that we have claimed for ourselves and that we have imposed upon other people. Yet tragically we are so often like the Pharisee in the parable that we cannot see our pride or hear our self-righteousness. And so Jesus gives us the example of the Pharisee who was too good to be true.

Too True to Be Good

The contrasting example in the parable is the publican who was too true to be good. He was, in fact, a man who was ruthlessly honest. He was a sinner and he knew it. He reflected his painful honesty in everything from his posture and gestures to his words. As I read his story I am amazed that he was at the temple, for that is not where one would expect to find a publican.

Publicans were not religious people. They were rejected by the religious community of their day. So I have to assume that something out of the ordinary had happened that drew him to the temple that day to pray.

Lyle Schaller writes about people who have been faithful in church attendance and who then become irregular in their attendance, or those who have been quite irregular and who suddenly begin to show up for worship services on a weekly basis or become involved even more deeply in the life of the church. He says that almost always it is an indication of some traumatic change in that individual's personal life. It's a turning point one way or another.

I suspect the same thing was true in the first century. The very fact that this publican was at the temple that day is an indication that he may have lost his job. Maybe the Romans had caught him embezzling funds. Or maybe he had discovered a whitened spot on his skin and suspected he might have leprosy. Or maybe he or his wife had had an affair. There was some great change in his life that brought him to God and brought him to the temple to pray.

He came that day knowing he was a sinner. You could tell it just by looking at him, even if you couldn't hear his prayer. For in those days Jews prayed differently than we usually do today. Unlike the man and woman in Westminster Abbey who got down on their knees and bowed their heads and closed their eyes and whispered their prayers, the Jews who came into the temple prayed in a standing position, not with hands folded in front of them, but with hands uplifted. Not with eyes closed but open, and not with heads bowed but raised toward heaven. I suspect that is precisely the posture in which the Pharisee prayed, but not the publican. The publican found a place over in a corner of the temple where he would be alone and where God would be the only listener to his prayer. His eyes were closed, and his only gesture was to beat his chest in agony over the anguish of what he had to confess. His prayer was simple: "God, be merciful to me a sinner."

> "God, be merciful to me the *sinner*."
>
> ❦

The literal translation of the Greek text is "God, be merciful to me *the* sinner." He also made a comparison. If you were to ask him how he compared to the Pharisee, he would have told you quickly that the Pharisee was the better man. He was the worst sinner of all. He had no hope, no righteousness, no good works—nothing but to come and throw himself upon the mercy of God and say, "God, be merciful to me the sinner."

Is his truth your truth? Against what backdrop do you measure your life? Do you compare yourself to the backdrop of God's perfect righteousness?

In moments of humility when we consider ourselves to be worse than anyone else we go to God and say, "God, you are my only hope.

My only chance is your mercy." If that truth is overwhelming to you, then listen to what Jesus teaches us about God's goodness: "I tell you, this man [the publican] went down to his house justified rather than the other."

What a stunning irony! The Pharisee, who thought he was so good, was judged by Jesus to be a pathetic sinner, and the publican, who thought he was so bad, was justified by Jesus to be good. The difference, of course, was a matter of personal trust. The Pharisee trusted in himself and his own goodness, and the publican had no trust in himself or his own goodness, but threw himself completely upon the mercy and goodness of God.

Jesus isn't concerned about who's praying. He is concerned about our eternal destiny. In this parable he is saying that those who depend upon themselves are fools who are eternally lost, while those who depend upon him and his mercy are wise and destined to eternal life.

Who are you in the parable—Pharisee or publican, proud or humble, self-righteous or depending on God's mercy? We may disguise ourselves and fool those around us, but there's no fooling God. God wants to know. Tell him about yourself. Confess your sins. Forsake self-righteousness. Say with the publican, "God, be merciful to me the sinner," for only in this way can we call ourselves friends of God.

Part Three

COMMUNICATION
AND COMMUNION

CHAPTER THIRTEEN

LOVING OURSELVES

William Shakespeare wrote in the first act of *Hamlet*:

> This above all: to thine own self be true,
> And it must follow, as the night the day,
> Thou canst not then be false to any man.

In other words, if a person has a right relationship with self, there will be a right relationship with others. In a way it is strange to talk about your relationship with yourself, but it is extremely important. Even though it's hard to define, it's something that we all intuitively know about. We recognize that all other relationships can end or be broken. You can outlive your parents, you can divorce a spouse, you can abandon your children or quit a job, but you can't end the relationship with yourself. It is the relationship that lasts for a lifetime.

WHO AM I?

Let's talk about our self-relationships in terms of three questions. The first is the question, "Who am I?" The answer to this is often shaped for us by others. The world constantly tries to define us by external appearances or by specific events in our lives, and that becomes our self-definition.

We're not the first to deal with this. Jesus dealt with the same problem. Some people said to Jesus, "I know who you are. You are Moses come back from the dead." Or "You're Elijah; you're Jeremiah." Other people said to him, "You're John the Baptist. He had his head cut off by King Herod, and you must be John the Baptist with his head put back on again." Or they said, "You're Beelzebub—the devil himself." Some called him the illegitimate son of a Roman soldier who had an affair with a young woman named Mary. They said he tried to cover it up with this virgin birth stuff. There were some who said he was a lunatic. People's identification of Jesus ranged from being a devil to being deity.

It is who we define ourselves to be that triggers the relationship that we have with ourselves. Unfortunately, there are a lot of inadequate definitions that people give themselves. Some people identify themselves as victims. Something clearly tragic happened ten or twenty years ago, and that has become the defining event of their lives.

Or people define themselves by their possessions. They think they are better than others because of their money, cars, houses, or businesses. The opposite happens, too, where people define themselves by what they *don't* have: "I'm the guy who doesn't own a house."

There are those who define themselves by their achievements, titles, or degrees. Some of us define ourselves in terms of our associations. In conversation we like to say who we know, because it makes us seem to be more important—as if the fame of others will rub off on us. Or we define ourselves in terms of the neighborhood or the place of employment or the church to which we belong.

Traditionally men have most often defined themselves by their occupations. Women have more often defined themselves by their relationships, but the list is long and varied. Different people answer the "Who am I?" question in many different ways. The problem with these common answers is that they are often faulty definitions. Money can be lost, youth doesn't last, and other people can break off their relationships with us.

So is there a Christian answer? Is there a different answer to the "Who am I?" question for someone who is committed to Jesus Christ as Savior and Lord? Indeed there is.

The best answer, the Christian answer, is "I am God's child in God's likeness." The Bible says I'm created in the image of God; that gives me a new understanding of myself that lasts forever. It is an understanding of who I am that no one can take away. A mugger can beat me up until you can't recognize me, but the image of God in me cannot be touched. I can lose all of the things that may seem to make me important or distinctive from other people, but when everything is gone I am no less a child of God. When I walk down the street, I don't have to think that I am young or that I'm old, that I'm educated or that I'm ignorant. All I need to know is that I look like God. I'm not God, but I look like him because his image is in me.

Just as there is often a resemblance between a child and a parent, there is a resemblance between a Christian and God. You can see it, you can hear it, you can sense the imprint of God on our lives. It's an indelible impression that lasts forever. It is better than anything else and of greater worth than all the other things combined.

You can sense the imprint of God on our lives.

For those who grasp what the Bible teaches when it talks about our being created in the image of God, it is life transforming. It revolutionizes the way we see ourselves, and that revolution carries over into all the relationships of life. A person who self-defines as a child of God can never have that taken away—not by robbery or rape or bankruptcy or failure. Being a child of God is better than anything else. There is no better self-definition than that "I am God's child created in God's image."

Galatians 3:26 and 28 say, "You are all sons of God through faith in Christ Jesus. . . . There is neither Jew nor Greek, slave nor free, male nor female, for you are all one in Christ Jesus." That is who I am, a child of God.

WHOM DO I LOVE?

The second question for a good self-relationship asks, "Whom do I love?" Love is the powerful fuel that makes a relationship good and strong and growing.

We know that if you love a child who is struggling with some deficit, love can make a miraculous difference. If a man and a woman deeply love each other, terrific problems and difficulties can drive them together instead of ripping them apart. Their love is more than fuel that drives them in each other's direction; it is like glue that makes them inseparable. If people around us are hurting, we know that if we love them, our love can transform them. The most eloquent words about love are found in 1 Corinthians 13:13, "These three remain: faith, hope and love. But the greatest of these is love."

Now put that together with what Jesus said in Mark 12:30–31: "Love the Lord your God with all your heart and with all your soul and with all your mind and with all your strength. The second is this: Love your neighbor *as yourself*." That's a strange thing to say. Does that mean we are to fall into romantic emotional love with God and everyone on the block? Of course not. Love is committed caring that acts out in the other person's best interest.

If I love God with all of my mind and soul and body and strength, that means I care so deeply for God that I will put everything I have into doing what is good for God. Loving my neighbor means that I will do what is best for my neighbor, even if she is unlovable and doesn't want anything done for her.

Jesus said, "Love your neighbor as yourself." Jesus assumed that we must love ourselves if we're going to be good at loving others. He's not talking about narcissism where people look in the mirror and think how great they are. It's not selfishness or greed or pride. Self-love is doing right for ourselves. If we really love ourselves we're not selfish; if we really love ourselves we are not greedy; if we really love ourselves we will not be proud, because those are not loving ways to be. In fact, true self-love is loaded with self-discipline, with righteous behavior, and avoidance of the sins that will wreck our lives.

Many times when we see people that we think are really in love with themselves, we have misunderstood. Often we're seeing self-*hatred*, for complete self-indulgence is highly self-destructive and can ruin a life. These people alienate themselves from God and everyone else, and it results in disaster.

> *We must love ourselves if we're going to be any good at loving others.*

A good self-relationship requires a biblical self-love, a love that comes up to God's standards. It is loving ourselves the way God loves us. It is treating ourselves the way God treats us. Imagine what this combination does for a person's life! Someone who says, "I'm not who everyone says I am—I am a child of God, and God's imprint is in me. I love myself to the point that I care for myself the way God cares for me. I treat myself the way God wants me to be treated." Can you imagine how healthy that is? Can you imagine what that does to the self-relationship that previously was struggling and self-destroying?

What Am I Supposed to Do?

That brings us to the third question: "What am I supposed to do?" If I am serious about this self-love, how do I get to the point where I can get along with myself? First, we need to accept responsibility for ourselves. That is contrary to the frequent messages in our culture. We live in a blaming society, and our culture is not one that easily accepts responsibility. When we run into a problem or a difficulty, we tend to quickly scan the horizon to find someone we can accuse of creating the problem. We blame our parents, our friends, our churches, and our employers. Currently the hot number one on the list of blaming others is to blame the government for whatever problem anybody has.

We live in a sinful and difficult world. Others do us wrong and we do others wrong, but at some point God calls us to accept responsibility for ourselves. Somebody may do me wrong, but that does not give me an excuse to respond inappropriately or unlovingly to that person. Somebody may treat me unjustly, but I am responsible for my reaction. I am responsible for my sins. I'm responsible for me.

When you think about it, this absolutely makes sense. We hear the same message through counselors, through twelve-step programs, and we've read it in the Bible. Galatians 5:19–21 tells us that we should take responsibility for the wrong we do, including "sexual immorality, impurity and debauchery; idolatry and witchcraft; hatred, discord, jealousy, fits of rage, selfish ambition, dissensions, factions and envy; drunkenness, orgies and the like." We need to accept responsibility for our own rage, for our own anger, for our own behavior.

The sum of this is that I can't blame you for my sins and problems. I have to take responsibility for myself if I am going to get any help. That is the self-loving thing to do. But if we hear only God's call to accept responsibility, we're in big trouble. We have all this responsibility piled upon us, and we discover very quickly that we cannot cope. That is why so many people don't accept responsibility. They can't handle it.

Responsibility is only the first item on God's list of things we are to accept. The second is to accept God's grace. Ephesians 2 in the New Testament calls upon us to accept the enormous generosity of God. When we quit blaming everybody else and take responsibility, we realize we can't solve our problems, and then we accept God's help—and he offers lots of it. God offers to forgive us no matter what we have done. He'll wipe the slate clean. He will give us grace to deal with whatever we face in life. He will always give to us whatever resources are needed in order for us to succeed and be all that he calls us to be.

Some people simply won't accept God's help. Some say, "I'm not worthy of God's help." That's right, none of us is worthy of it. There are others who are quick to say, "I can do this myself. I don't need help from God." That is such a misunderstanding of reality that it is hard to know how to respond. It is arrogant pride.

We are to accept responsibility and to accept God's grace, and then add a third: to accept our own uniqueness. You are *you* and I am *me*, and we are different. That's a great truth from God. Every one of us is unique, completely different out of all of the billions of possibilities.

God is very clear on the fact that we are each one of a kind. Each of us is part of God's greater whole and each of us is specially designed and has great value. When we accept our uniqueness it is transforming, for all we need to be is ourselves. I don't have to compare myself to you anymore. Age, height, race, or gender—these don't make any difference. I am me and you are you. We don't have to compete—it's silly to do so. When we accept the uniqueness that God has given to us, then we can all be what we were meant to be in the bodies that we have, in the intelligence, race, gender, and age that God has granted to us.

Put all that together, and we are ready to grow. We're ready to grow in our relationship with God, in our relationship with ourselves, and in our relationships with others—as we'll explore in the next several chapters. It is a basis for healthy relationships all the way around. It's a great way for me to be me and it's God's marvelous design for you to be you!

CHAPTER FOURTEEN

THE SHARING LIFE

St. Jude Children's Research Hospital in Memphis, Tennessee, received a plain white envelope in the mail. Inside was a game piece from the McDonald's Monopoly game that was being played at the time. The piece had printed on it simply: "One million dollar instant winner."

Whoever sent this to the hospital included nothing else in the envelope. There was no return address on the envelope, and the only clue to who sent it or where it came from was the postmark from somewhere in Texas. An interesting sidebar is that the fine print in the game rules stated that you could not transfer the ownership of a winning piece from one party to another; doing so invalidated it and McDonald's didn't have to pay. However, some wise person in public relations at McDonald's decided that it probably was a good idea in this case and they would pay. As a result, St. Jude Children's Hospital receives $50,000 a year from McDonald's over a period of twenty years. Someone in Texas decided that it was better to share than to be a millionaire.

Another news story played out in suburban Minneapolis. One December all 280 employees of the Rollerblade company received a Christmas card from former owner Bob Naegele and his wife. Along with the Christmas card was a check made out to each employee. The amount of the check was $160 for every month that they were employed by Rollerblade. For some employees it was a very significant amount of money—in excess of twenty thousand dollars. There were no hooks, no conditions, and no accountability as to how the money was to be spent. This was a free gift, with the taxes paid in advance so that the whole amount went to the employee. The total cost is estimated to have been about one-and-a-half million dollars. There were reports of the employees' excitement, surprise, laughter, tears, and joy when they received these checks.

I was particularly interested in the closing paragraph of a Minneapolis *Star Tribune* story. It tells about a conversation between Matt Majka, the director of product marketing, and Bob Naegele. Majka said, "You can't imagine the impact you have had on everyone." And Naegele replied, "That is just what I wanted to hear. This is not mine. It is a gift I had to share."[1]

These are stories of enormous generosity, but they're nothing compared to the greatest story of sharing—the ultimate example. Unmatched and unsurpassed. It is the story of Jesus Christ sharing his riches with us, his friends. Second Corinthians 8:9 says, "You know the grace of our Lord Jesus Christ, that though he was rich, yet for your sakes he became poor, so that you through his poverty might become rich."

As Rich As Heaven

Speaking of rich, Jesus was really rich. As rich as heaven—owner of earth and the entire universe. He was in heaven as comfortable and

---

[1]The Minneapolis *Star Tribune*, December 1995.

content and wealthy as could possibly be.

It's interesting to think about that and to imagine what he was like. Riches do different things to different people. Sometimes when people acquire a significant amount of wealth they want to hoard it, always thinking up ways of getting more. By contrast, other people take great delight in what they have received and are anxious to give it away or to share it with other people. They consider themselves blessed and they want the blessing to go around.

The story of Jesus hints that there's nothing wrong with riches. The clear implication of the Bible is that Jesus was as rich as anyone could possibly be and there was nothing at all wrong with that. The issue, of course, is what a person decides to do with whatever riches he has.

Jesus decided he wanted to share his riches with us. We can almost imagine him sitting comfortably in heaven one day dreaming about what he could do with his exorbitant wealth. His great dream was to share his wealth with us. He decided he was willing to leave heaven and come to earth, becoming poor himself—in order to give to us. You know, it's got to be incredibly difficult to become poor if you have been the richest person of all. Jesus decided to become poor in order to give what he had to us and to make us as rich as he is.

What does all of that mean for us? It means that Jesus loves us a whole lot more than anything he owns. It also means that everything that we have comes from him. We usually don't think of it that way. We think that we have worked very hard, or saved very carefully, or our success is the result of a good education, or that we simply lucked out and ended up with a lot of good stuff. But if the riches originate with him, then everything we have, whether it's a job or money or good health or possessions or relationships—all of these riches are because of his generosity. It means that we should never be proud, because what we have didn't come from our own efforts. It means we don't need to hold on to things with a tight grip, because he will take care of us. It also means that the greatest expression of wealth is not money but salvation, because that is the main reason that Jesus came—not to enhance the balance in our bank accounts, but so that we could have eternal life. He wanted us to come to live in his heaven, to be in the presence of God, to experience the very best of the best.

When Jesus came he had a fabulous secret he wanted to share. It is one of those wonderful truths that changes the lives of those who get it. Jesus had to decide the best way to communicate this fantastic secret of his. He could use a deductive approach, where he would tell about it and then show how it's done with an illustration or an example. Or he could use an inductive approach, where he would show how it's done with the hope that we would figure it out for ourselves before he told us about it.

The greatest expression of wealth is not money but salvation.

Let me explain the difference. In my high school chemistry class we were studying the Periodic Table of the Elements. When we came to sodium, the teacher wanted us to learn that it is a comparatively unstable element. Instead of turning to the chalkboard and writing "Sodium is an unstable element," he had an experiment for all of us to share. Each pair of lab partners took a Petri dish and put some water in it. Then one person from each team received a very small sliver of sodium from the teacher and put it in the water. Wow! That little piece of metal really whipped around that dish! I was impressed. From that observation we were supposed to figure out for ourselves that sodium is not a very stable element.

I remember very little about high school chemistry. I don't remember the teacher's name. I can't recite the Periodic Table, and I remember very few of the abbreviations for the elements. But I do remember that sodium is an unstable element. Not because the teacher told me but because the teacher showed me.

JESUS' GREAT SECRET

Jesus chose the inductive approach to tell us his great secret. He could have just told us, but he showed us. I should mention that he didn't always use this teaching approach. Sometimes he used the deductive approach. When it came to the dangers of sin he knew it was best to warn us instead of letting us find out for ourselves and suffer the inevitable and awful consequences.

So what did Jesus show? He showed great generosity. He loved people who hated him. He forgave people who never even asked to be forgiven. He healed people of terrible diseases who after they were healed walked away and never turned around to say thank-you. He befriended people whom no one else would have anything to do with—Gentiles, poor people, prostitutes, and criminals. He did not try to accumulate wealth—he never owned a house or a business or a vehicle of transportation. When he stood before a Roman governor on trial for his life, the clothing that he wore was not his own. He died on a borrowed cross and was buried in a borrowed grave.

In Acts 20:35 Paul says to remember "the words the Lord Jesus himself said: 'It is more blessed to give than to receive.' " At the very center of the Christian life is this wonderful secret: The best way to be happy is to give.

To be a Christian is to be a sharer!

To be a Christian is to be a sharer! It is to be like Jesus Christ. Christians are those who share their time and their gifts and their love and their money and themselves. We have received so much from Jesus that we want to do exactly what Jesus did and share with as many others as we possibly can.

I want to tell you that it works. There are those who are lonely and friendless and anxious in life because no one seems to care about them.

When they use their little bit of emotional reserve to reach out and befriend someone else they often are helped themselves. There are people who are frazzled because they can't get everything done. They have no time to give to anybody else because life's plate is so full and the schedule is so packed. Yet taking a few minutes to reach out to someone else can have a revolutionary effect on one's schedule. There are those who struggle with finances, and no matter how much money they make there never seems to be enough to pay their bills. But when they start to give some money away, it has a transforming effect on the entire management of their finances. The best way to solve our problems is to share with others whose problems are bigger than ours.

To say this is dangerous. Someone may start sharing for selfish reasons. There may be people who say, "That's great! I want to be happy. I want to get more money. I need more time. I've got all these problems to get solved, so I'm going to start sharing." But that's selfish and counterproductive. That's not what it's all about. The best approach is to be like Jesus and do what he did to discover from experience that it really is "more blessed to give than to receive."

Jesus shared himself with us selflessly and with gracious humility. Follow his example and share the riches of life he has given you with others, and do so humbly, knowing all you have has come from him.

CHAPTER FIFTEEN

IMPERFECT PEOPLE

Sometimes we have terribly unrealistic views of reality, particularly within the lives of our Christian brothers and sisters. Our sensors are always tuned in to other people and we develop perceptions about them. Sometimes we conclude that other people are perfect. We think to ourselves, "Life is easy for them. They are healthy, happy, and financially secure." But others might be perceiving us in just the same way. And we know things are far from perfect.

Remember the Thessalonian Christians whom the apostle Paul boasted about? At the time he wrote his first letter to the Christian church of Thessalonica, Paul didn't perceive that it was a gathering of boastworthy people. To the contrary, he perceived that the people he saw were people with problems. He saw some with severe financial difficulties, not just a current crisis, but a chronic situation for all of their adult lives. Some had too much money, some had too little money, and some merely mismanaged their finances whether they had too much or too little. He looked at others and saw that they suffered from addictive behaviors. He looked at couples and recognized that while at times there was the appearance that everything was fine, in truth there was constant stress between them that occasionally blew up. It was so painful that they didn't want to speak of it to anyone else.

There were those who had serious doubts about God and about Scripture. They had some fundamental reservations that hardly could be spoken to other people who seemed to believe everything so easily. He saw other people who came to the church desperately looking for friendship and not finding it. He looked and saw some with the fabric of their family tearing apart, some who had chronic pain. He saw all kinds of people with all kinds of problems and he was burdened for them.

Paul looked beyond the appearance of togetherness and perfection on the outside to the reality of the problems that he understood everyone to have on the inside.

One day when he was thinking of the Thessalonians and all their problems, God's Holy Spirit spoke to him and gave him a revelation. It was an insight to understand what the church of Jesus Christ is all about. It is not a gathering of perfect people; it is not even a gathering of adequate people, but rather it is a coming together of people with problems, weaknesses, stresses, and struggles. It is a gathering of people who do not have the answers, but who come together in the name of Jesus Christ seeking those answers. It is a group of people who gather together to experience God—to be helped and to help, to be healed and to heal. It is a group of people who provide for one another by meeting their problems.

Having received a revelation from God, Paul provided a context for the solution of problems in a single sentence:

> We urge you, brothers, warn those who are idle, encourage the timid, help the weak, be patient with everyone. (1 Thessalonians 5:14)

Warn the Idle

Paul lays out before them four specific actions that they can take. He starts the list by saying, "Warn the idle." Paul uses a Greek word of military origin, referring to a soldier who was out of step with the rest. While others were taking a left, that soldier was taking a right. That soldier was to be warned that he was not in step with all the rest. When Paul talks to the Thessalonians, though, he's talking specifically about those who have their lives out of order not with other Christians but with what God wants for Christians. He says that they have to be warned.

The idle are not to be condemned, but to be warned.

Examples of this are many. Some are out of step with God in their financial lives. There are others who are out of step with what God wants in their sexual behavior. Some Christians are out of step with God's will in the things they speak. They are quick to criticize and sometimes caustic in their words. These people are not to be condemned, but to be warned. They may not even realize that they are out of step with the rest. We are to warn others when their lives are out of order and also warn them about the possible consequences.

The word Paul uses here not only refers to being out of step but also includes those who wouldn't work—those who were idle. Some people are out of step with what God wants in terms of their employment. He is not talking here about leisure, but about loafing. He is talking about people who refuse to get regular jobs, who refuse to provide for their families, and specifically to those who turn to other Christians and expect them to provide for them in ways they are not providing for themselves. We need to understand clearly who is being spoken of here. It is not someone who has been laid off; it's talking about someone who simply refuses to work.

The refusal to work may have all types of guises. It may be someone who speculates on a get-rich-quick scheme and says, "Don't worry, my ship is going to come in, I'm going to be loaded," but refuses to work in the meantime. Or it may be someone who borrows against a future inheritance, yet refuses to be productively employed while waiting for the inheritance to come. God is saying that such persons are to be warned that their lives are out of step with what God wants.

I don't know about you, but I find it rather difficult to walk up to somebody, tap him on the shoulder, and say, "Just let me warn you, you are lazy and you need to get to work." How do you say those things? How do you say it when you hardly know someone? It may be even more difficult to say it to someone you know very well.

A friend of mine had chest pains, was admitted to the hospital in the afternoon, and went through a battery of tests. Late that evening, he was in the cardiac care unit talking with the cardiologist who said, "We need to schedule you for heart surgery first thing tomorrow morning. In fact, we are reordering the surgical schedule for the day so that you can be on the top of the list." He then handed my friend a consent form to be signed.

My friend replied, "This is all new information to me; I need some time to process it. I need to take a few days to think about this, to pray about it, and to talk with my family and decide what to do." Just as he was saying this, his family physician and personal friend, who had been informed of the test results by the cardiologist, stepped into the room and overheard this conversation. He interrupted, saying, "Darrell, you don't have time. You must have the surgery first thing tomorrow or it will be too late." And so my friend went ahead with the operation and recovered marvelously—all because he had a friend who cared enough to warn him, to tell him where he was in relationship to where he needed to be.

That is what we're to do as fellow Christians. Within the Christian community, there are some who need to be warned that their lives are out of step with God. For us to fail to warn them makes us guilty of spiritual malpractice. We need to tell them what they need to hear so that they will be able to get back in step. That is Paul's first action in providing for fellow Christians with problems.

ENCOURAGE THE TIMID

The second action is to "encourage the timid." Although it doesn't quite make sense to us, timid literally means "those who have small souls." What it really means is those who are discouraged—very discouraged. It seems to me there are two basic reasons why people could be described as small souled, or timid. Some individuals are born that way. Their makeup is such that they are frequently discouraged. They are often down in the pits and have extreme difficulties coping with life. It is hard for them to get up the courage to go on another day or even another hour.

Other people experience discouragement because of specific circumstances. Perhaps they've gone through the death of parents, the struggles of a divorce, sudden unemployment, or a frightening diagnosis, and for that day or year they have become timid or fragile. The apostle tells the Thessalonians that it is those who are fragile that we are to encourage. They need to be lifted up. They need someone who will come alongside, maybe in their own inadequacy, and prop them up, speak a word, give some help, do what needs to be done so that they can be encouraged. They are not to be condemned, even though they may have brought their present circumstances upon themselves. Even though they may have done things that have made life difficult for them, they need someone who will stick by them, someone who will care, someone who'll be tender and understanding. They need someone who'll give encouragement to their small souls.

Isaiah 42:3 is a verse I have always loved. It's often used to describe Jesus, but is really applicable to any servant and follower of Jesus Christ. It says, "A bruised reed he will not break, a smoldering wick he will not snuff out."

If you walk through the woods and come upon a sapling that an animal or vehicle has run over, without thinking about it, you snap it off and go on your way. Or, if you see a lantern where the flame has gone out and it is just smoldering, you turn it down all the way—put it out and be done with it. The servant of the Lord is one who does not break the bruised reed and does not put out the smoldering wick, but rather encourages and props up that which otherwise might break off and lights anew that which otherwise might go out. Encourage the timid.

Help the Weak

The third action Paul tells the Thessalonians to take in providing for fellow Christians is to "help the weak." The church is the place for the weak, for those who do not have power. I'm not sure I can adequately explain to anyone who has power what it is like not to have power. Power is what enables us to get what we want in this world in relationship with other people. It is expressed in a thousand different ways.

If you have money in your wallet right now, you have power—power that others who do not have money simply do not have. You have the power to purchase, the power to influence, and the power to control, whether you use it or not. And someone who does not have it is materially weak and powerless. If you have a job and someone else does not have a job, you may not understand the powerlessness and weakness of being unemployed. Power comes in the form of the clothes we wear, the cars we drive, the insurance we carry—all those different things are forms of power. It is only when we face a situation where we don't have the money, we don't have the influence, we don't have whatever it takes to change the situation to enable us to cope—it is then and only then that we understand what it means to be weak and to be powerless.

There are a lot of people who have no power, who are weak, whose calls aren't returned, and whose problems aren't solved. It is those people who are weak who come to the church of Jesus Christ as a place for help. And it is here that we have committed to help the weak, to come alongside them, to provide the time, the money, the counsel, or the understanding. It is the church of Jesus Christ where the weak will not be abandoned. It is the church of Jesus Christ where those who are weak and powerless are to be accepted and aided even when they have nothing to offer in return.

We are to be eager to help those who are powerless.

It is a recurring theme in Scripture that the strong are to help the weak. The rich are to supply for the poor. The healthy are to heal those who are sick. Now, don't misunderstand what is being said here. I am not suggesting that those who are lazy ought to be provided for in their refusal to work. I'm not suggesting that people who are manipulative and seek to take advantage of others should not be confronted. The church of Jesus Christ is pictured in Scripture as a gathering of those who are weak coming together and finding their strength in the Lord God himself. We are not to criticize or condemn, but to be eager to help those who are powerless.

There is a special note that I need to insert here, and that is that we avoid the temptation to institutionalize what we are being urged to do. Sometimes we have a tendency to avoid personal responsibility and say, "The church ought to handle that," meaning that we call the church office or we expect someone who is in an official position of leadership to help, encourage, visit the sick, or do whatever needs to be done. But that is not what is being said at all. Even though we are in the midst of our own struggles and our own problems, we are to take it as our own responsibility to help the weak.

BE PATIENT

The apostle goes on to add a fourth action that ties in with all three previous actions: "Be patient with everyone." Problems require patience.

Our society has deceived us into thinking that there is a quick solution to just about anything. If we're sick, we take a pill and think we'll be well. If we have a spiritual problem, we talk to God and expect a quick answer. Most other societies don't think that way.

In this high-speed, high-tech society we have little patience in understanding that some problems in life take years to solve; some are never solved. We may not like it, but it's true. Problems require patience. We need patience concerning our own problems and patience concerning the problems of other people.

Problems also require a diagnosis. Have you noticed that the instructions Paul has given, "to warn the idle, to encourage the timid, to help the weak," all assume a correct, prior diagnosis? What happens if we *warn* the timid instead of encourage or if we *help* the idle instead of warn them? Then we are compounding someone's problem. Then we are taking the discouraged and stomping them into the ground. Then instead of warning the idle, we're enabling them to remain idle and out of step. So we must first have a correct diagnosis. We need to take the time to understand one another well enough to see what the problem is and to pray for wisdom from God. Even more important, we must allow God to take his time in our lives and in others' lives, so that if God chooses to take years to work, we don't rush in where God has chosen to delay. Scripture also urges us to be patient with everyone, and that includes those who get under our skin, those who test and aggravate the normal limits of our patience.

I invite you to look for people with problems, imperfect people. I urge you to warn those who are idle, to encourage the timid, to help the weak, and to be patient with everyone.

CHAPTER SIXTEEN

WALKING THE WALK

Thousands of years ago, the playwright Sophocles wrote the Greek tragedy *Oedipus*. It is the mythical story of Oedipus, the son of Laius, the king of Thebes.

Oedipus went to the city of Thebes that was being terrorized by a Sphinx. The Sphinx told a riddle to all who walked by, and if the riddle was not correctly answered (no one had answered it correctly to that point), the Sphinx would kill and eat the person who had been unable to answer the question. The city of Thebes now had no king, and it was offered that anyone who could answer the riddle and defeat the Sphinx would be the next king of Thebes.

Oedipus heard the riddle for the first time when he came before the Sphinx: "What animal goes on four feet in the morning, on two at midday, and on three in the evening?" Where others could not answer, Oedipus correctly answered, "man." In infancy, man crawls on all fours, and then at midday, or adulthood, man walks on two feet, and in old age, he walks with a cane, making for three feet.

Oedipus was victorious over the Sphinx because he was a keen observer about the way people walked. Just as God is a keen observer of the way we walk. He carefully observes every step we take and, in so doing, is able to understand who and what we are in our relationship to him. That is why he included in the Bible these words:

> It has given me great joy to find some of your children walking in the truth, just as the Father commanded us. And now, dear lady, I'm not writing you a new command but one we have had from the beginning. I ask that we love one another. And this is love: that we walk in obedience to his commands. As you have heard from the beginning, his command is that you walk in love. (2 John 4–6)

All of those words can be simply summarized by saying that we are to walk Christianly. If we claim to be friends of Jesus Christ, then that is the way we ought to walk, reflecting the relationship that we have. Let's look at our own walk as we consider three steps in these three verses.

WALK IN THE TRUTH

First, God commands Christians to walk in the truth: "It has given me great joy to find some of your children walking in the truth, just as the Father commanded us."

The words here are somewhat cryptic, for John was writing at a time when the persecution of Christians was increasing, and he didn't want to identify who they were, perhaps jeopardizing their lives. So he identified himself in the first line of the letter as "the elder." He was an old man, almost one hundred years old, but more than that he was a spiritual father of many of the Christians of that day. The "dear lady" to whom he refers is the church that he was addressing, and her "children" were the Christians who were part of that Christian community.

Speaking these words as a father, John takes delight and joy in the walk of some of the Christians in that church. John was expressing something that I think is not unusual as persons mature and change their perspective on life. It seems to me that when we are younger and more competitive, we have a strong desire to prove ourselves and are particularly interested in our own success. But as we grow older and become more mature, there is an even greater satisfaction in the success of others and particularly in the success of those whom we dearly love. That is why John takes special delight in the joy that he has over Christians who walk in the truth.

What specifically did he find in this church? Well, he found people who loved God and wanted to live for him. He found people who had committed themselves to Jesus Christ, who wore the name Christian, and desired to live for Jesus. That is not to say that they did not have problems or troubles, just as we do. Most of the problems we face are universal. They transcend culture, language, geography, and time. They, like we, struggled with jobs, getting along with the boss, financial troubles, politics of the day, dangers of war, strain in their marriages, and tests in their relationships with children and parents. They had troubled friendships, worries about health, and all the problems everybody faces, and yet John found that they still walked in the truth.

Those Christians knew they lived in dangerous and difficult times, but they still walked in the truth.

They chose their steps carefully, even though it was like walking through minefields. A misstep could blow them up. Those Christians knew that they lived in dangerous and difficult times, but they still walked in the truth, carefully following God's paths and God's patterns—even when it was uncomfortable and even dangerous.

This old man writing the letter found joy in them, and I understand that. I understand because I, too, am a pastor and I find tremendous joy in seeing Christians who—in all of the realities of life, in all the pains, in all the problems, and all of the tension—choose the right path. Sometimes it is easy and sometimes it is with great pain and sacrifice, but they make that choice and successfully do it. It is a great source of joy to watch Christians as they take their path through all of their experiences month after month and year after year, walking in truth.

When John writes that "some" do, he clearly implies that "some" don't." There are Christians who know what's right, but choose what's wrong. They have read the map, but choose their own way instead of God's path of truth. Just as those who "do" cause joy, those who "don't" cause sadness. Not anger, but sadness. Any parent who has a child with great potential and who goes the wrong way experiences sadness. John experienced sadness that there were only some who walked in the truth.

One year I spoke at a conference in Northern California at the Asilomar Conference Center. It is a magnificent place, right along the Pacific Coast. The facilities were grand, the weather was wonderful, and it was just a terrific experience.

Between sessions one day, I had a couple of hours free and decided to take a walk through the sand dunes and along the beach. When I crossed the road and came to the sand dunes, I came face-to-face with large signs explaining how fragile and delicate and damaged the sand dunes are along the Pacific Coast. Because the damage is caused by people, the State of California has created laws and penalties for walking outside of the marked paths. As a result, I stayed on the path, and discovered that it went over bridges, through the sand dunes, up onto the cliffs overlooking the Pacific Ocean, and along the coast. It was a delightful path to take. I saw wonderful sights and heard tremendous sounds. For the most part it was easy. Occasionally there were some shortcuts I would have liked to take, some places I would have liked to go, but I chose to stick with the path, and it was a wonderful experience.

As a Christian I try to walk through life the same way—always following the path of truth. It also is a clearly marked path, for God tells us in the Bible that we are to do it his way and explains the reasons why. God has marked the path quite clearly and has given laws and penalties for those who leave the path and go their own way. For those who stick to the path there is sometimes inconvenience, but, for the most part, it is an easy path. True, sometimes it goes around a long way when we would prefer to take a shortcut, goes to places where we would not choose to go, or misses places where we would like to go, but in every case, it is the right path that we as Christians are to follow. It is wonderful to walk in the path of God's truth. That is what walking Christianly is all about—walking in the truth!

LOVE ONE ANOTHER

The second step of walking Christianly is explained in verse 5: "And now, dear lady [or dear church], I am not writing you a new command but one we have had from the beginning. I ask that we love one another."

Suppose for a moment that you were asked to write down the main command of God that would summarize everything else. Which of the many commands in the Bible is the most important? I can tell you that at Asilomar the big command was "Keep Off the Sand Dunes!" But God's command is not so negative. To the contrary, it is the most positive command that there could be. God's big command is "Love one another."

John carefully points out that this is not a new idea he thought up; it is as old as God himself. This is the "original recipe," and it cannot be changed. This original recipe of love goes back to God. It is the main thing that he wants us to do. And so loving one another is the primary characteristic of a Christian walk.

Some years ago I went to visit a man in a hospital who was scheduled to have surgery the next day. I walked down a long corridor, and as I entered the room the family gathered around the bed laughed and said they thought it was me! It turned out that as they listened to the sound of my footsteps coming closer they had taken a quick vote and had come up with a unanimous decision that it was me.

Now, I never thought my gait was all that unique, that people could identify it without even seeing me, but I think that is a lot like the Christian walk. God can tell a Christian's walk—it has the sound of love.

We need some clarification here on what God means by love. There is often a great deal of misunderstanding. For the most part, people would say that love is an emotion; it is a feeling of attachment, of affection and loyalty that we have toward another person. It seems strange to be commanded to love, because we

God can tell a Christian's walk—it has the sound of love.

think that our emotions aren't controllable. We feel that love is just there or it isn't there, and it is kind of nonsensical to imagine being commanded to love someone that maybe we don't even like. While, to be sure, emotions are important, we have to understand that when God speaks of love, he speaks of love as being a choice that we make. It is choosing to care for others. It is choosing what's best for the other person. It is loving others as God loves us.

If love is defined as good actions rather than emotional feelings, and everyone chose to love that way, then everything in the world would be revolutionized—from neighborhood squabbles to the resolution of the Middle East crisis.

Unfortunately, we know from thousands of years of history that everyone is not going to choose to love, especially when it is hard to do. But Christians do choose love. In obedience to God's command, we choose to love, and that is the way we walk Christianly.

OBEDIENCE TO GOD

Now add the third step of how to walk Christianly: "And this is love: that we walk in obedience to his commands. As you have heard from the beginning, his command is that you walk in love" (v. 6).

Here and elsewhere the Bible teaches that love and obedience are so tightly connected that they are inseparably linked.

God is saying, "Don't say you love me and then disobey me. That's a contradiction." If we say that we love him, we should obey him. We should behave in a way that is consistent with the Word, and if we don't, our words are not true. This isn't talking about making some stupid mistake; it is talking about deliberately choosing to do wrong. Most of the time we know what God wants and commands. Doing it demonstrates our love. Disobedience says we don't really love God at all.

Just as love means obedience, so obedience means love. The Christian who says, "I choose to obey God" must also choose to love others, because they are inseparably linked. Hardly a day goes by when we are not given the choice of treating someone rightly or wrongly. At work or at home, talking on the telephone or to people at church, no matter what the context, there is a constant flow of events where we may choose to love other people. Others may put us down or break our hearts, but we are to choose to behave toward them the same way that God has chosen to behave toward us. Every time we love (especially those who don't deserve it and are not very lovable), we demonstrate our obedience to Jesus Christ.

Every time we love we demonstrate our obedience to Jesus Christ.

Think of these two Christian virtues with every step you take: love and obedience, love and obedience, love and obedience. The two linked together is the way that we walk like Jesus Christ.

We started with a riddle from a Sphinx. Let us finish with a riddle from Scripture.

There are people in the church and in the world who claim that they are Christians. Some of them walk Christianly and some of them don't. Here is the riddle: How do you tell which is which?

You can find the answer in the words of 2 John 4–6.

CHAPTER SEVENTEEN

LOVING OUR NEIGHBOR

In the words of Mister Rogers:

It's a beautiful day in this neighborhood,
A beautiful day for a neighbor.
Would you be mine?
Could you be mine?
It's a neighborly day in this beauty wood,
A neighborly day for a beauty,
Would you be mine?
Could you be mine?
I've always wanted to have a neighbor just like you!
I've always wanted to live in a neighborhood with you.
So let's make the most of this beautiful day:
Since we're together we might as well say,
Would you be mine?
Could you be mine?
Won't you be my neighbor?

Won't you please,
Won't you please?
Please, won't you be my neighbor?[1]

Mister Rogers of children's television fame is not the first one, or the only one, to say that neighbors are among the most important of relationships in life. One day a very long time ago a Pharisee came to Jesus with a question:

> "Teacher, which is the greatest commandment in the law?"
> Jesus replied: " 'Love the Lord your God with all your heart and with all your soul and with all your mind.' This is the first and greatest commandment. And the second is like it: 'Love your neighbor as yourself.' " (Matthew 22:36–39)

A LONG TRADITION

Jesus spoke to an important Jewish tradition of treating your neighbor right. It went all the way back to Moses and the Ten Commandments: "You shall not give false testimony against your neighbor. You shall not covet your neighbor's house. You shall not covet your neighbor's wife, or his manservant or maidservant, his ox or donkey, or anything that belongs to your neighbor" (Exodus 20:16–17).

Even alien neighbors were to be treated well. According to Old Testament Jewish law:

> When an alien lives with you in your land, do not mistreat him. The alien living with you must be treated as one of your native-born. Love him as yourself, for you were aliens in Egypt. (Leviticus 19:33–34)

I'm often impressed that the Bible, although an ancient book set in

---

[1]©1967 by Fred M. Rogers. Used by permission.

a different place and time and culture, is amazingly relevant and up-to-date. One of the biggest issues facing our country today has to do with how we treat those who are foreign born—those who are aliens. The Bible's simple advice is to consider foreigners as neighbors and to love them. It reminds us that we, or our ancestors before us, were also foreigners and aliens.

The Bible's simple advice is to consider foreigners as neighbors and to love them.

Unfortunately, by the time of Jesus many among his people had lost the Old Testament concept of what it meant to rightly treat a neighbor. For example, the Roman soldiers, who had come and conquered the land, were hated by those who had been conquered. They defined the Romans as non-neighbors and therefore treated them miserably. The axiom of the day was that if you came across a Roman soldier who was sick or wounded, you should let that soldier die so there would be one less Roman to fight against. There were some who expanded that to all Gentiles. It was commonly understood that if a Gentile woman was having difficulty in childbirth you should let her suffer and die, for then there would be two less Gentiles for you to worry about.

Neighbors increasingly became defined as "our kind of people." Neighbors were people whom we liked and who were like us—people that shared our values. But it was not just a first-century Palestine tradition; it has been done repeatedly in every generation, in every ethnic group, in every country including in America today.

A lawyer came to Jesus one day with a legal question. "Who is my neighbor?"

In reply Jesus said: "A man was going down from Jerusalem to Jericho, when he fell into the hands of robbers. They stripped him of his clothes, beat him and went away, leaving him half dead. A priest happened to be going down the same road, and when he saw the man, he passed by on the other side. So too, a Levite, when he came to the place and saw him, passed by on the other side. But a Samaritan, as he traveled, came where the man was; and when he saw him, he took pity on him. He went to him and bandaged his wounds, pouring on oil and wine. Then he put the man on his own donkey, took him to an inn and took care of him. The next day he took out two silver coins and gave them to the innkeeper. 'Look after him,' he said, 'and when I return, I will reimburse you for any extra expense you may have.' " (Luke 10:30–35)

Then Jesus asked,

"Which of these three do you think was a neighbor to the man who fell into the hands of robbers?" The expert in the law replied, "The one who had mercy on him."
    Jesus told him, "Go and do likewise."(Luke 10:36–37)

A New Definition

With that story, Jesus changed the definition of a neighbor from *who that person is* to *what I do in relationship to other people.* The issue is not whether a person is a Jew or a Gentile or a Samaritan; black, brown, or white; rich or poor, a good guy or a bad guy. It doesn't matter whether he got himself into the trouble. For it could well be argued that anyone who lived between Jerusalem and Jericho knew that was a dangerous road infested with bandits, and this was what you could expect if you traveled alone without a caravan. But that didn't seem to be considered. Whether he was capable of repaying wasn't a factor. The definition of a neighbor is in me—it's what I do to help others. Not who they are or what they do. The difference is both astonishing and transforming.

As Christians, it means that we are no longer reactive. Our side of the relationship to neighbors is not based on who they are or what they do. My relationship to someone else is based on the way I behave, not the way that person behaves. It's based upon who I am as a Christian.

Jesus demonstrated proactive love in revolutionary ways. He did things that left other people very uncomfortable. He was kind and generous to Roman soldiers. As a result he was accused of acts of treason. Jesus invited and allowed women to become part of his core of disciples at a time when rabbis were not even supposed to speak to women. He welcomed children to his side, to sit on his lap, when his closest friends and followers shooed them away. He even touched lepers, who by law had to cry out "unclean" so that everyone could keep a distance.

Jesus demonstrated proactive love in revolutionary ways.

When Jesus said that Christians would become known for their love, he envisioned the church with love flowing both ways. Not loving because the love is deserved, but loving because the love of Jesus Christ flows through us.

What does it practically mean? It means that we may use this love of Jesus Christ as the most powerful instrument in relationships. It is not dependent on other people, for we can't control other people. Other people will always do things that we don't like or that we don't agree with. If we are not bound by their behavior but instead bound by the love of Jesus Christ, then we can impact the lives of others as Jesus did. It may be the way we drive. It's letting other people pull into line. Maybe it's by standing in as a parent or even being a surrogate daughter or son! Or it might be sending an anonymous gift of money to someone experiencing financial difficulties—just to demonstrate the love of Jesus Christ for that person. Or maybe you have a professional skill that you could donate to serve the poor. Would you be willing to give a half-day, or a day, or maybe a week's vacation to provide that professional skill for someone who needs it?

Do these things not in reaction to what others have done, but based on the love of Jesus Christ, which has filled us up and now overflows so that we can love our neighbors as ourselves.

Speak for Jesus Christ when you say to others:

Won't you please,
Won't you please?
Please, won't you be my neighbor?[2]

---

[2]Ibid.

CHAPTER EIGHTEEN

CHRIST AT WORK

We Americans ask each other three standard questions in order to get acquainted: "What is your name?" "Where do you live?" "What do you do?" For many people, the most important questions of all is "What do you do?"—as though all of life is defined in terms of job or occupation. We pick up with great interest the list in the newspaper or *Money* magazine that tells which are the most prestigious jobs in America—what the starting pay is for each position and the median and the high. When I list six different occupations, it's a safe guess that you will have an automatic rating system for the prestige and pay of all six of them: the CEO of a Fortune 100 company, a public school teacher, a neurosurgeon, a used car sales person, a migrant worker, a movie star.

There's no doubt about it, in America our jobs say a lot about us. We define ourselves so often in terms of our occupation that our job has become one of life's most important relationships. Of all your waking hours, if you are a typical American, 60 percent of them will be spent on the job. We do our work more than any other single thing in all of life. If relationships at work are good, that goes a long way to making life pretty good. And if relationships at work are bad, that can spoil much of the rest of life.

A Biblical Job Description

The Bible says a great deal about work. It gives great advice on how we as Christians can relate to our jobs. What the Bible does *not* do is make a big deal out of job titles or job descriptions. The emphasis is not so much upon what we do as how we do it.

Let's take a look at Colossians 3:22–4:1. Paul, the author, wrote the words to a different time and a different culture, covering the whole range of all of the jobs in society from slave to master. He says,

> Slaves, obey your earthly masters in everything; and do it, not only when their eye is on you and to win their favor, but with sincerity of heart and reverence for the Lord. Whatever you do, work at it with all your heart, as working for the Lord, not for men, since you know that you will receive an inheritance from the Lord as a reward. It is the Lord Christ you are serving. Anyone who does wrong will be repaid for his wrong, and there is no favoritism.
>
> Masters, provide your slaves with what is right and fair, because you know that you also have a Master in Heaven.

There's an underlying assumption in the Bible that whatever job we have in the whole range from slave to master, we should assume that God has called us to that job and that we should live our Christianity in that occupation. Even slavery! That's a very different approach from common thinking in America, where we assume that the only way we will ever be happy and fulfilled in life is if we do exactly what we are wired to do and want to do.

Does that mean the Bible is telling us that if we have a terrible job we have to stay with it until we retire—for the rest of our working life? First Corinthians 7:20-24 speaks directly to this issue.

> Each one should remain in the situation which he was in when God called him. Were you a slave when you were called? Don't let it trouble you—although if you can gain your freedom, do so. For he who was a slave when he was called by the Lord is the Lord's freedman; similarly, he who was a free man when he was called is Christ's slave. You were bought at a price; do not become slaves of men. Brothers, each man, as responsible to God, should remain in the situation God called him to.

This passage is talking especially to the new Christian, who is told to stay in whatever job he or she had when becoming a Christian. It's also saying that if you can get a better deal, then go for it! Let's say you're a slave in the first century and your master becomes a Christian and offers you your freedom—you should take it. In other words, the Bible is telling us, whatever your present position, assume that you're there because God cares. He's involved in your life. That's where God has put you, and you should stick it out unless God provides an opportunity for something better. Now, obviously that doesn't mean you should continue doing something that is evil or wrong. It doesn't apply to professional bank robbers and Mafia hit men, or similar jobs! But it is to say that when we have a position that is in the normal range of human occupations, we should live out the call of Jesus Christ in that context.

The Bible advises: "Whatever you do, work at it with all your heart as working for the Lord, not for men" (Colossians 3:23).

In other words, whether slave or master, migrant worker or CEO, it is not so much the job that is important, but how we do the work we do in the job we have.

A fascinating story is told about a man who was negotiating to buy a house, and because of circumstances he never went to see the house.

The day came for the closing, and he actually signed all the papers and bought the house, site unseen. A friend and business advisor told him that was a strange and excessive risk to take. When asked why he took such a risk, he answered, "Yes, but I know the man who built the house, and he builds his Christianity in with the bricks."

As Christians, we are to work Christianly no matter what we do. Our jobs are a primary means for us to live out all that it means to be a follower of Jesus Christ. Christianity is not primarily something that we do when we gather together with other Christians on Sunday morning. What being a Christian is all about is how a person builds a house, or answers the phone, or manages the home, or programs the computer, or treats the patient, or manages the apartments, or deals with difficult customers, or teaches the students, or works at the job of finding a job during unemployment.

Our jobs are a primary means for us to live out all that it means to be a follower of Jesus Christ.

Paul told the Corinthian Christians, "Whatever you do, do it all for the glory of God" (1 Corinthians 10:31). The "glory of God" refers to God's reputation. Whatever the job I do, my job is to enhance the reputation of God in the way I do that job.

You may hold the most menial and unpleasant of jobs in society, and therein you have the opportunity to show heaven and earth the way a Christian lives and works to make God look good in the worst of circumstances. Or you may have one of the most prestigious and comfortable jobs in all of America; that is your opportunity to show heaven and earth the way a Christian lives and works to make God look good in the best of circumstances.

You may say, "You don't know my job. For one thing, I am underemployed. My education and my background and my experience make me overqualified for what I am doing. The people I work with are anything but Christian. They are anti-Christian in many of the things they say and do. My job is really tough!"

Set thoughts of your job aside for a minute and imagine what it was like for Jesus in the carpenter shop in Nazareth. He probably spent most of his time building cabinets for the homes of the people in his community—cabinets, and perhaps wooden yokes for oxen that were used to plow the farmers' fields. In his previous job he made stars and planets and universes, mountains and trees, sunsets and sunrises. He was highly overqualified for working in a carpenter shop. He went from master Creator to apprentice carpenter. But I suspect that what he did in both of his jobs was to work well to make God the Father look good, to enhance his reputation. He made God look good with his creation of mountains and galaxies and magnificent sunsets, and he also made God look good in the sturdy chairs and well-constructed tables and yokes that he made. As Christians our model is Jesus. Whatever we do, wherever we do it—let us do it like Jesus would.

THE CHRISTIAN'S REAL BOSS

We are going through a profound restructuring of business in America. With downsizing and mergers, acquisitions and layoffs, and rapid high-tech advances in so many industries, we can no longer expect that we're going to have lifetime employment in a company. Business expert Peter Drucker says that what we are now seeing in America is the move to functional self-employment. At best, we are all just temporary employees of businesses and really work for ourselves. Others complain that they work most of the year for the government just to pay their taxes. Many are slaves to debt. They feel that between their mortgage and credit card debts, they work primarily for the bank or the credit card companies. And then there are some loyal employees who say they work for their manager. The most important thing for them is to make their boss happy.

Imagine instead, when you go to work tomorrow, that Jesus is your boss. For he is really the only boss a Christian worker has to please. Think of it this way: Jesus got me the job, so nobody can fire me without his approval. Jesus is the boss, and he is delighted when I serve him well, but disappointed when I mess up. Jesus is 100 percent committed to my success. He wants me to be both effective—doing the right things—and efficient—doing them in the right way. Jesus is my boss, and his reputation is on the line when I answer the phone, design a product, balance a ledger, tutor a child, fly an airplane, or do anything else. Jesus is the kind of boss who wants me to learn and grow, who stays close enough to help and supervise, but lets me develop my independent creativity without reining me in too much. He's committed to my success. He trusts me enough to give me hard assignments—things that I would never want, working with people that I would never choose—because he knows that's good for me. He is a great boss to work for!

And he pays well. One of the basic rules of a job interview is that your first question should not be about the pay. There's a subtle transaction that goes on when you're being interviewed. You're supposed to convince the employer to like you, and if she does, then let her bring up how much the pay is. It's not that we don't care—it's just the protocol through which we must go.

Jesus trusts me enough to give me hard assignments.

Those first-century Christians were told to work for boss Jesus: "Since you know that you will receive an inheritance from the Lord as a reward" (Colossians 3:24). God knows that pay isn't everything. Research shows that if somebody is extremely well paid yet hates his job, the money is not enough. In fact, there are a lot of people who will switch jobs and take a pay cut in order to increase other aspects of job satisfaction. God also knows that we like to get good rewards. He's the one who created us. He knows how we think and how we function, and he promises to benefit us by sharing his wealth with us.

No one is richer than God. He pays very well. He gives to us an inheritance. Inheritances generally are deferred income—they are a ways off, even in heaven. But inheritances can also begin paying out early, can be distributed here and now.

A man I know was offered a job in Minnesota for an organization twice the size of the one he currently worked for. He was somewhat disappointed when the new employer never asked him his current salary. He was simply offered a salary package—take it or leave it. What his potential employer did not know was that it was just one hundred dollars more than the man's current salary. He made a decision to take the new job and moved halfway across the country for it. It didn't quite make sense. But when asked how he made that decision, he said that he made it not on the basis of the numbers, but on the basis of his expectations. He was convinced that his new employer, far more than his old one, would do what is right, would give regular raises, and in the long run he would be far better off.

The same goes for our pay when we work for Jesus. It may seem at times as if we could do better if we worked for ourselves. If we did it the wrong way instead of Jesus' way we might be ahead, at least for the short term. But if you really trust Jesus to be the good and great God and Savior that he is, you come to the conclusion that you are working for someone whose resources are unlimited. His love and concern are unmatched, his inheritance for us in heaven is infinite, and his grace to us here on earth is always adequate. We need not worry, for we can always trust Jesus to do what is fair and good and right.

WHAT IS YOUR ASSIGNMENT?

Imagine God calling a meeting of all Christians. He's up front, telling us his vision for the future of the world. He says that he dreams of having his representatives in every country of the globe. We will represent him and work together with him to accomplish his great purposes for humankind.

Then God starts making assignments. The excitement runs high. He says, "This group over here goes to Germany; you over here are assigned to France. That group goes to Belize, and this section goes to the United States." There is a group that goes to the People's Republic of China, and another group is assigned to Bolivia. He divides us up all around the world.

Our group meets with God, and he explains that now that we have our territory, we are to work for him to demonstrate what it means to be a Christian in all the different circumstances of life. He tells us, "I want you to represent my Son, your Savior Jesus, and show everyone what it's like to be a Christian, independent of the varying circumstances. I would like some of you to live with superlative health and show the world that even though you are strong and healthy you still depend upon Jesus. Others of you, I'm going to trust with pain and a prognosis that is at best uncertain, so that you can show faithfulness to me even when you do not have what everybody desires. To some of you I am going to give great wealth, so you can show everybody that it won't turn your head or your heart. And some of you will live on the edge of poverty to show the world that you are still loyal and faithful and that you have a joy that transcends even the things that you do not have. Some will have difficult marriages, others romantic delights. Some will have children and some will be childless. I want to be represented everywhere."

Finally, God assigns us to specific jobs. Contractor. Store manager. Homemaker. Physician. Counselor. Stockbroker. Volunteer. Accountant. Designer. Teacher. Writer. Self-employed. Unemployed.

What's your assignment? What did you get? What matters most is not the job you got. What matters most is the work you do and the boss you serve, so that whatever your job, you do it well as an employee of God, as a representative of Jesus Christ. Whether a slave or a master, "whatever you do, do it all for the glory of God."

Part Four

AMITY AND
ENMITY

CHAPTER NINETEEN

HOLY AND SEPARATE

Our generation has overwhelmingly emphasized the "softer side" of God. We are very familiar with talking about God in terms of God's love, God's mercy, God's patience, and God's kindness—all things that are the softer side of God. At the same time we've neglected what might be called the harder side of God. Actually that's not good terminology because it makes it sound as if God may be inappropriately harsh or maybe even horrible. What we really should say is that we have tended to neglect the *holy* side of God.

If we get down to the basics of what everybody should know about God, one of the things that must be included on that list is that God is holy. The word *holy* is found 584 times in the English Bible. That tells us that holiness is important in the Bible, although perhaps not well understood. My guess is if we took a quick poll, a lot of Christians would have some difficulty defining exactly what it means to be holy. Holy in its root meaning means to be separate or distinct. The idea is that God is separate from everybody else. He's one of a kind. However, the difference primarily relates to evil. God is completely distant from anything and everything that is evil.

Too Pure to Look on Evil

The Old Testament prophet Habakkuk gives us a graphic description of God: "O Lord . . . your eyes are too pure to look on evil; you cannot tolerate wrong" (Habakkuk 1:12–13).

We don't really understand God until we understand how different and distinct he is from anything that is evil or bad or sinful. God can't even look at it. We could say that God is allergic to evil. He's allergic to sin.

I have never suffered from common allergies, but I've observed many who are allergic to pollen, chemicals, or animal dander. It's a big deal! It can impact all of your life and make you sick. I do have a serious reaction to poison ivy, which is more of a sensitivity, and really not an allergy. Call it what you want; let me tell you, I hate the stuff!

I remember being covered with a poison ivy rash when I was in the seventh grade. I missed three weeks of school. I had it on the bottoms of my feet, on my hands, in my mouth; my eyes were swollen almost closed—it was a terrible experience! One arm was so swollen that for almost two weeks I was unable to bend it.

But you know, I learned a lesson. I learned to stay away from poison ivy. If I see it, I go in the opposite direction. If I mow the grass and see any poison ivy, after I'm finished I take a shower to make sure that I get those oils off me. I would be glad if poison ivy were obliterated from the face of the earth! I know of no socially redeeming value to poison ivy. So when it comes to poison ivy, I'm "holy"—that is, I'm separate from it. I want nothing to do with it.

God has a far greater aversion to sin than I do to poison ivy or than you do to anything that makes you sick. God hates sin. He doesn't even like to look at it. He doesn't want to have anything to do with it. It would be fine with God if sin were obliterated from the face of the earth and out of the universe. There is no redeeming value to sin. So God is separate. God is holy.

However, we misunderstand the holiness of God if we see it only in terms of what God is against. We need to understand that holiness is more than God being separate; it has to do with God being superior. That's a hard concept for us to grasp. This is a different kind of superiority than God's power or knowledge. When we say that God is all-powerful, we are saying that he has supernatural power greater than all the might of the military of all the nations of the world. His power is greater than all the nuclear weapons that could ever be exploded. When we talk about God's knowledge, we mean that he knows more than everyone in the world knows or every computer knows. God's knowledge infinitely exceeds all the information we have.

The holiness of God means that God is morally and ethically superior to the very best of us. God is the purest of the pure. Isaiah 6:1–5 is a report of the experience that the Old Testament prophet Isaiah had when he received a glimpse of heaven.

> In the year that King Uzziah died, I saw the Lord seated on a throne, high and exalted, and the train of his robe filled the temple. Above him were seraphs, each with six wings: with two wings they covered their faces, with two they covered their feet, and with two they were flying. And they were calling to one another: "Holy, holy, holy is the Lord Almighty; the whole earth is full of his glory." At the sound of their voices the doorposts and thresholds shook and the temple was filled with smoke.
>
> "Woe to me!" I cried. "I am ruined! For I am a man of unclean lips, and I live among a people of unclean lips, and my eyes have seen the King, the Lord Almighty."

Did you notice that the celestial seraphs were awestruck by God? What they talked about was not how much he knew or how powerful he was. They were struck by his holiness. Those who encounter the holiness of God are shocked by his purity and his superiority. The holiness of God is dazzling.

For the angels of heaven, the dazzling thing about God is his character. More than anything else, God has impeccable integrity. He is morally and ethically perfect. In fact, holiness is a number one characteristic of God.

The holiness of God is dazzling.

If you could make a list of every characteristic to describe God and rank them in order of importance, the first would have to be God's holiness. Holiness is more about what God is than all of his power and all of his knowledge.

WHO IS LIKE GOD?

The bottom line is that God is unique. He is one of a kind. In about 1500 B.C., Moses wrote, "Who among the gods is like you, O Lord? Who is like you—majestic in holiness, awesome in glory, working wonders?" (Exodus 15:11). The obvious answer is that no one is like God. No one is as holy as he is. No one is as majestic.

We've done an interesting thing in everyday English. We've watered the word *unique* down to mean something that really is not akin to the true definition of the word. We tend to use the word unique more to say that something's unusual or special. We frequently put adverbs in front of it: "It was a really unique experience"; "She is a totally unique person"; "What happened was very unique." We really shouldn't put a modifier with "unique," because "unique" means that it is the only one in its category. There are no others. There is nothing to compare to. Something can't be very unique. If it's unique, it's the only one. It can't be really unique; it can't be totally unique.

That's who God is. He is unique. He is one of a kind. No one else is like him. His uniqueness is primarily in his holiness. He is so good. So perfect. So right. So opposite of evil. So contrary to sin. God is holy. But we're not. We're sinners. All of us.

The Bible has a very pointed statement in Romans 3:23 that says, "All have sinned and fall short of the glory of God." Or another way of saying it is, if we compare each of us to the holiness of God, every one of us comes up short by comparison. Nobody measures up to God.

When you were a kid did you ever stand on the shore of a lake and throw stones to see who could toss them the farthest out into the water? Let's imagine that a group of us line up for a contest like this. We'll imagine we're on the North Shore of Lake Superior. Everybody gets to pick six stones, and we all take our turns. And by the way, the objective is to hit Sault Ste. Marie in Ontario—about four hundred miles directly across Lake Superior.

The first person really winds up and lets go. The stone makes it about twenty-two feet out into the water. Bad news. The next person makes it out a hundred yards. Everybody says, "Wow! That's really good." But then you remember the target is four hundred miles away on the other side of Lake Superior.

That's the way it is comparing us to God. If the rock toss were a morality contest, a mass murderer could probably only throw his stone about six inches, while Mother Teresa might have heaved her rock an impressive four hundred feet. That's great until you realize that the target is on the other side of the lake. She fell short. We all fall short of this holiness of God. What is really crazy is the way we can sit around and talk about how good a toss we made. "I got 117 feet." "Wow, you're good!" But that's not good! It's not good when the target is the other side of the lake. The point is not how far we made it, but how far we missed. The standard for holiness is God, and our best shot isn't good enough. It's totally inadequate.

When we realize the holiness of God, we echo the words of Isaiah,

"Woe to me! I'm ruined! For I am a man of unclean lips, and I live among a people of unclean lips, and my eyes have seen the King, the Lord Almighty." I've seen the goal. I know how high it is. I know how spectacular and holy is the Lord God Almighty.

SEPARATED FROM GOD

If God is holy and if we are not, if God is allergic to sin and sinners and we are sinful, that means that we're separated from God. That gets very serious. That means that while we want God to be our friend, the truth is he's allergic to us and we've become his enemy. It means that when we want to be close, God has to keep a distance. It means that while we want to live forever in his heaven, he just can't have us there. He can't have us in heaven if we're sinners because he can't stand to be around sin. And then we begin to see that our lives become lousy and our eternity is destined to be an eternity without God.

When we understand our situation, we begin to despair. We start to whimper and say, "Is there no hope? Does this mean that we are forever stuck—that we can never get close to God?" That's where the good news comes in. When we are at our lowest point there comes this bright shining light and a clear voice speaks the gospel. Gospel means good news. It is the good news of Jesus Christ—the good news that we do not have to be alienated from a holy God. We can be holy as well!

Think of it as if we are in a courtroom in the district of heaven. God is the judge on the bench and we are the defendants. We are sinful. We say with Isaiah, "Woe is me. I don't have a chance here. I'm doomed." And then up steps the Son of God, Jesus Christ. He offers a deal. The deal is that he will come to earth, die on the cross, pay the price of sin, and there will be an exchange. The exchange is that our sin will be transferred to him and his holiness will be transferred to us. God says, "Yes." So Jesus came and died and Jesus rose again from the dead and completed his side of the offer.

Then God says to us, "All you have to do is step up to the railing and accept the deal." Some do and some don't. Those of us who do accept the deal are "born again," as John 3 calls it. It's the transfer of the holiness of Jesus Christ to us. It is when we agree to become saints.

Do you know what "saint" means? It means "holy one." So anyone who agrees to this deal that is offered becomes a saint. When a person becomes a Christian she or he is legally reclassified from sinner to saint in the records of heaven. It is an instant and permanent transaction.

However, it can take a lifetime for the practical change of holiness to take place. The practical change is that we become like God. Not like God in that we have infinite power. Not like God in that we have infinite knowledge. But like God in that we are separate from sin.

It can take a lifetime for the practical change of holiness to take place.

Think of it this way. Suppose you're broke and you are deeply in debt. I mean serious debt—a million dollars in debt. You know that in your lifetime you would not have a chance of ever catching up. Then someone gives you a billion dollars; it will be transferred to a trust account in your name. It's in an irrevocable trust, so it will never be taken back. It's yours. Technically at the moment the wire transfer takes place you are a billionaire, but you don't quite have it yet. You still owe a million dollars.

What you do need to do, of course, is start making withdrawals from the trust. You start paying off the money that you owe, and you start living like the rich person you have become.

That's sort of what happens when we become Christians who follow Jesus Christ. We are legally holy, but it takes time to withdraw from our account of the holiness of God, to stop sinning and to start acting like the holy persons that God has declared us to be.

There's a powerful line in the New Testament in 1 Peter 1:15–16: "Just as he who called you is holy, so be holy in all you do; for it is written: 'Be holy, because I am holy.'" God is saying that we are to be holy the way he is.

Let's go back to the poison ivy for a minute. As I've gotten older, because of my terrible experiences with poison ivy, I avoid it. If I see a clump of poison ivy, I go in the opposite direction. If I am near a fire where I think that they're burning weeds that might have poison ivy in them, I'm going to get as far away from the smoke as I can. I intentionally avoid anything to do with poison ivy.

Those who are holy increasingly do the same thing with sin. We've been burned by it. We've had the blisters and the problems. We know the consequences, and whenever we see it we want to step back and avoid it and be separate from it. That's what it means to be holy as God is holy.

If we only know a few things about God, this is one of the things we must know—that God is holy. And the more we see his holiness the more in awe of him we become. The more we see his holiness the more we are aware of our sinfulness. And the more we choose to leave sin behind the more we'll become holy like God and our friendship with him will grow.

God, we stand in awe of you. You are unique. You are pure. You are holy. Forgive our sin. Make us holy through Jesus Christ our Lord. Amen.

CHAPTER TWENTY

A SUFFERING WORLD

A passenger ferry capsizes in the harbor of Port-au-Prince, Haiti, drowning scores of innocent people. An AIDS epidemic goes through central Africa taking the lives of tens of thousands of adults, but also condemning children to death from the day they are born. A young mother is diagnosed with inoperable cancer and is shaken, not so much by the prospects of the disease and death, but by the realization that she won't be there for her children and the fear that when they grow up they won't remember her. TWA flight 800 inexplicably explodes just off the coast of Long Island, taking hundreds of lives and leaving grieving people in France, the United States, and elsewhere who have lost their best friends, their loved ones, or their closest relatives. A godly woman whose one great desire in life is to be a mother sits in the physician's office and is told that she is infertile and she will never bear children.

The list goes on like the names in a big-city phone book. Global calamities and personal private tragedies are everywhere. In every generation every person suffers, some sooner, some later, some lesser, some more, but no one's exempt, no one is excluded. Pain and suffering are part of every life.

Where is God when we hurt so much? If it is true that God is great and that God is good, you would think that he would not allow there to be such difficulty in our world. Why doesn't he use his goodness and his power to call a halt to all of the maladies of our world? Why doesn't he just step in and make the huge difference that he is capable of making? Doesn't it sometimes seem as if, at best, God is under-qualified for his job? Or that he is, at worst, some type of celestial sadist who takes actual pleasure in the problems that we ordinary people face? It really is no wonder that some people object to believing in such a God. To believe in God seems to them to compromise the most basic convictions of goodness, justice, and mercy.

The question of how a good God could allow so much suffering in the world is a very real objection, a genuine concern, a reason why people choose not to become Christians or become bitter, resentful Christians. It is such a serious problem that to be completely honest, it is difficult to answer to everyone's satisfaction. Maybe it is difficult to fully answer to anyone's satisfaction, but as a Christian I'd like to try.

Why Does God Allow Suffering?

To give an explanation that is acceptable and reasonable, perhaps the place to start is with an honest admission. It's true that God allows great suffering in our world. How could that be hidden? All you need to do is look around. It raises a pair of questions. First, the why question. Why does God allow suffering? And then in some ways the more important question is, what does God do about this suffering? The question of why there is such great suffering in our world is not a question that is limited to Christianity. It's a question that needs to be addressed by every religion and by every philosophy in the world. The person who says, "I'm not going to become a Christian because I don't want to believe in a God who allows so much suffering in our world" has not ended the issue. He can reject Christianity, but he still hasn't answered the question of why is there so much pain and suffering. Why is there such injustice? What's his reason, his explanation? Where did it come from? Why isn't our world automatically good? Why isn't it pain-free?

What about the conclusion of the Hindus, who say that everything ill that we suffer in this life is a consequence of sin in our previous lives? If an individual has "bad karma" from a previous life there isn't anything to do about it except wait until he dies and somehow hope for a better chance the next time around.

What if someone chooses to become an atheist and doesn't believe that God exists? How does she explain pain and suffering and injustice? It just is? It just exists? All the problems of this world and this life lead to death—and when it's over, there's nothing more?

Christian answers are not necessarily simple. They can be complex. Actually, there can be multiple answers. Many reasons could explain why God allows suffering in our world. I won't suggest that this is a complete list, but let's consider three possible reasons.

The first reason has to do with the teaching that God has created us with human responsibility. True responsibility always comes with consequences. God could have done it differently. He could have made us into robots programmed to worship him. We'd be programmed to keep the Ten Commandments, to always say the right thing at the right time.

As human parents we would rather have a real live baby than a doll that says, "I love you" when we pull the string. Real babies don't always giggle when we want them to giggle, they don't always say, "I love you" when we want them to say, "I love you." They don't always do what we had expected them to do when they grow up. But that's the way we want it to be. We don't want our children to love us just because they were programmed to love us, and we don't want our friends to be our friends just because they were made to be our friends.

So it is that God gave us choices. We were given the responsibility to love God or to hate God. We were given the responsibility to manage our environment. We were given the responsibility to make choices, because God wanted us to choose what was good and right and not just be controlled.

Our ancestors made some very bad choices. They chose against God and they chose for sin. By so doing, they contaminated our human race and our whole world. The consequences have been awful: wars, diseases, broken relationships.

When I was in the eighth grade we all had to do projects for math class related to ratios and the practical use of them. One girl baked a cake using ratios to alter the recipe to be large enough to adequately serve everyone in the class. She brought this big cake to class, explained how she had used ratios to make it, and said we could eat it, which we thought was great. The teacher, asked, "How are we going to divide the cake into seventeen equal parts?" A boy raised his hand and said, "I can do it, I know how!" The teacher said, "I don't think you can." This boy was absolutely sure he could and came up front. He took a big knife and began to cut up the cake. The more he tried, the worse it got, until he finally looked at the teacher and said, "You're right—I can't cut it into seventeen equal parts." What he did was wreck the cake. It was a total mess and everyone in the class did not get a fair share—just globs and pieces. It wasn't fair what he did to the project and it wasn't fair what each one of us got.

That's a lot like what's happened to the world. We humans were given choices and we have cut up God's creation in combinations that have left the world an unfair place with a lot of things that are not the way they originally were intended to be. We were so sure we could do better than God that we proceeded until we ruined the whole project.

We're all in this together. What one of us does tends to affect all of us. Just as one person can contaminate a public water system for everyone, the evil behavior of other humans can and does impact us all.

The Bible sums it up in Romans 5:12: "Sin entered the world through one man, and death through sin, and in this way death came to all men, because all sinned." This is saying that the responsibility for sin and evil and suffering and pain in our world is ultimately ours, not God's.

Although our responsibility is a primary factor, there are other factors as well. The second reason is that God is engaged in a great battle against his archenemy, the devil. Satan's story is woven throughout the Bible and throughout our own experiences. A classic example of it is the Old Testament story of Job, who was attacked by Satan in an attempt to discredit and displease God. Satan took the lives of all of Job's children, stole his wealth, and caused disease in Job's body. First Peter 5:8 says that "the devil prowls around like a roaring lion looking for someone to devour." He devoured Job's life and he still does it to people today.

That is not to say that all the suffering in our world is because of Satan. Our human sin would be sufficient to cause all of the misery that we could ever imagine. But the reality is that God is involved in this great conflict against evil. We are on the battlefield, often wounded by what happens. It is a real war.

Wars not only have casualties but they also have lingering effects. The spiritual battle in our world between God and Satan has continued to leave terrible consequences. The pain and suffering inflicted by God's enemy is horrendous.

A third reason to consider as a source of suffering in our world involves God's divine purposes. Sometimes God either allows or causes pain and suffering in our world and in our lives to accomplish good purposes that wouldn't otherwise happen. It may be to get our attention or to stop us from doing something that is wrong. Many times

> *The pain and suffering inflicted by God's enemy is horrendous.*

unless difficulty comes our way we may pursue a course that is inappropriate. Sometimes God has to bring us up short. He may use pain to discipline us for sin.

The Bible has many stories of individuals whose lives were interrupted by the intervention of God in painful ways so that he could stop the evil that they were doing. God may cause us to lose a job we very much wanted because he knew that in the future that job might lead to criminal activity. Or he may allow us to suffer a painful broken relationship rather than marry the wrong person. It could be that God touches a nation with financial reverses, diseases, or famine in order to accomplish his greater purposes.

Hebrews 12:6 says, "The Lord disciplines those he loves"—just like a parent. That may explain some of the suffering that is in our world. However, all of the explanations eventually go back to the primary concept: God has given us responsibility, and responsibility leads to consequences.

WHAT DOES GOD DO ABOUT SUFFERING?

Even if we don't completely understand why God allows suffering, the most practical question for us is "What does God do about suffering?" Most of all, God knows and he cares. Isaiah 53:3 describes Jesus as "a man of sorrows and familiar with suffering." Luke 19 tells us that Jesus looked over the city of Jerusalem and was so gripped by the difficulties of the people that he wept. In the book of John we're told how Jesus was summoned to the side of his friend Lazarus who was terminally ill. Jesus didn't get there until Lazarus had died. When he heard the news of Lazarus' death, he was so overcome with grief that we have the shortest verse in the English Bible. John 11:35 simply states: "Jesus wept." He was touched by human pain and sorrow. So never think that God doesn't care. He does care.

William Barclay was a Scottish journalist and a New Testament scholar whose heart was broken by a tragic event. His daughter, who was soon to be married, went out sailing with her fiancé in the North Sea off the coast of Scotland, and in a terrible boating accident both of them were killed. To add extra suffering to the pain, their bodies were never recovered. William Barclay wrote, "The day my daughter was lost at sea there was sorrow in the heart of God."[1] God knows and he cares.

God cares enough that he has used his power to limit evil. God puts restraints on how far our responsibility and freedom of choice can and will go. For if he didn't, if he let sin and evil run its full course, we would be destroyed. We would destroy our world.

There's a little book in the Old Testament called Lamentations; it is the lament of the Jewish people in hard times. Lamentations 3:22–23 says, "Because of the Lord's great love we are not consumed, for his compassions never fail. They are new every morning." The assumption is that if human evil could run its full course, we'd be consumed by it.

> *"Because of the Lord's great love we are not consumed, for his compassions never fail."*

Some people will say, "If God can apply limits, why doesn't he fix it so that by noon tomorrow all sin and evil would just be obliterated off the face of the earth?" Wouldn't that be great? But wait a minute. We have all sinned. We're all guilty of evil—not just what other people do to us. It's inside of us, and it's what we do to others as well. If that's the case, then by noon tomorrow we would all be obliterated. You see, the good news is that God cares enough to give us responsibilities and consequences, but he does put an outer limit on what could be. I think that if somehow we were able to step back and get a broader eternal perspective, what would amaze us is not how much suffering and pain there is in the world, but how comparatively little there is because of the grace of God

---

[1]William Barclay, *A Spiritual Autobiography* (Grand Rapids, Mich.: William B. Eerdmans Publishing Co., 1975), 46.

and the limits that he has placed. God has stopped the very worst. He has limited evil.

The greatest act of God in answer to human suffering is that he sent his Son. It is all summed up in John 3:16–17: "For God so loved the world that he gave his one and only Son, that whoever believes in him shall not perish but have eternal life. For God did not send his Son into the world to condemn the world, but to save the world through him."

God made the ultimate intervention when he sent his Son to transform us so that we can choose to do good instead of wrong. There's a sense in which it is a blatant offense to God to say, "God, why don't you do something?" when he's already done it. He's done the greatest thing that he could ever do—he gave his own Son to come to die on the cross to deal with the problem of human evil.

The good news just keeps getting better. In Revelation 21:1–4, God gave a preview of history so that we could anticipate what is to come. John wrote,

> Then I saw a new heaven and a new earth, for the first heaven and the first earth had passed away, and there was no longer any sea. I saw the Holy City, the new Jerusalem, coming down out of heaven from God, prepared as a bride beautifully dressed for her husband. And I heard a loud voice from the throne saying, "Now the dwelling of God is with men, and he will live with them. They will be his people, and God himself will be with them and be their God. And he will wipe away every tear from their eyes. There will be no more death or mourning or crying or pain, for the old order of things has passed away."

CHOICES

As we observe and experience the very real suffering and pain in our world and in our lives, there are three choices we can make. We can reject God, we can resent God, or we can trust God. Those who reject God have nothing left. They have no good explanation for what's happening in our world and, worst of all, no hope.

Far more common is to resent God. Something goes terribly wrong. Someone you love has awful pain or a tragic death. You experience harsh disappointment and say, "Where were you, God? You could have done something. You could have stepped in, and I resent you for not using your power for my benefit." Resentment turns a person bitter and angry, often alienating that person from the love of God that can cause the healing that is needed.

You can reject God, or resent God, or trust God. Trusting God is believing that he is good and wise even when we cannot adequately and fully explain all that is going on. Even though we are in the midst of pain and suffering that we hate, we have absolute confidence that God knows what he's doing and is trustworthy—no matter what.

We each have a choice. That's the way God made us. We can even choose what to do with God. Reject him, resent him, or trust him. The choice is ours.

CHAPTER TWENTY-ONE

THE HYPOCRITICAL CHRISTIAN

Many people have a negative response to Christianity for unfortunate reasons. They have had bad experiences with Christians, and as a result have rejected the Christian faith. The objection is most often stated in the simple accusation that Christians are hypocrites. That's a serious accusation. Because, after all, if Christianity doesn't work to transform the lives of those who are already Christians, then what are the chances that Christianity can transform the lives of those who are not yet Christians?

Sometimes the objection is based on that which is quite trivial. Someone misspoke, and that has been exaggerated over a period of years until it has been turned into an excuse rather than a genuine reason. More often, there has been misbehavior, hypocrisy, or something far more serious. Unbelievers may say, "I know some Christians who have done some terrible things. My boss talks about Christian faith a lot, but he has become a very rich man by underpaying his employees and taking advantage of other people who are far less fortunate than he is. If that's what a Christian is, then I don't want to be a Christian."

Then someone else joins in the conversation and says, "Frankly, that reminds me of my mother. Everybody thought she was this super holy saint. Everybody around the neighborhood and in the community would tell me what a great privilege it must be to have her as my mother. But at home she was mean, she was vindictive, unpredictable, and terribly cruel." Another person adds, "Yeah, like my father. My father was a leader in the church, but at home during the week he would beat up my mother. He would beat up me. Sometimes we wouldn't go to church on Sunday mornings, because we didn't want people to see the bruises and to find out what he had done." The conversation continues, and the accusations become more serious. Another person adds, "Well, in the church in which I grew up, the pastor would preach these wonderful sermons, Sunday after Sunday. Then after all these years they discovered that he had been molesting boys in the Sunday school and youth group. He was caught and sent to prison."

Then everybody joins in and says, "And what about these celebrities, these famous religious leaders who it turns out are having affairs or stealing money or ripping off the savings of poor elderly people with their fund-raising solicitations?" Or "What about the fact that some of the greatest racist atrocities have been committed by people who claim to believe in Jesus Christ, and have said what they have said and done the horrible things they have done under the banner of the cross of Jesus Christ? And what about the people who say they are Christians but in private repeat the ugliest jokes and the worst slurs?"

Who in their right mind would believe in Christianity if that's the way Christians are?

A RESPONSE TO OBJECTIONS

As a Christian, I want to respond. For starters, it is important to talk about what a hypocrite actually is. A hypocrite is a pretender. Our

English word *hypocrite* comes almost letter for letter and sound for sound from the Greek word for a stage actor. Someone on the stage is a pretender. He or she pretends to be someone that the actor is not. In this case we're not talking about someone who is on the stage in a theatrical performance. We're talking about someone who is pretending to be in real life what that person is not. The person accused of being a hypocrite may not be a Christian at all. It may be that the misbehavior is so unchristian because the person is *not* a Christian.

We can look at this another way. A hypocrite is a counterfeit, and that which is a counterfeit is an attestation to that which is real. Obviously, counterfeiters don't make seven-dollar bills, because there is no such thing. Counterfeiters don't typically make one-dollar bills because they have such minimal value. The most commonly counterfeited U.S. currencies are twenty-dollar bills and one-hundred-dollar bills. If the real thing doesn't exist, it is hardly worth faking it. The fact that people fake being Christians is because Christianity is real. It is worth trying to copy.

At the same time, it is important to confess that Christians are sinners. It is impossible to become a Christian without first admitting to being a sinner and confessing that sin to God. After all, Christians are those who say that Jesus Christ is our Savior, and the only person who needs a Savior is someone who is a sinner. If a person is not a sinner, obviously there is no need for salvation, so Christians are those who have turned to Jesus Christ to be saved from their sin.

Unfortunately, the sin does not stop at the moment that a person becomes a Christian. It is not as if God reaches down and turns off the faucet of sin. It may be turned down, it may be reduced, but it is a lifelong process, where we sin less and less and become more and more like Jesus Christ. First John 1:8 says, "If we claim to be without sin, we deceive ourselves and the truth is not in us." Anyone who's a Christian—and these words are written to Christians—and claims to be without sin, is a liar. The remedy is in verse 9: "If we confess our sins, he is faithful and just and will forgive us our sins and purify us from all unrighteousness."

The Bible explains that any Christian who claims not to have sinned is a liar. A real Christian is someone who has accepted Jesus Christ as Savior, and has been born again. His or her life has been transformed, and the problem of sin has been resolved as far as heaven is concerned, but the problem of sin in this life on earth will take some more time. That doesn't mean that Christians are supposed to sin. The Bible never says that. However, we do sin, and therefore God has provided a way to clear that sin through confession of it and acceptance of God's forgiveness.

Getting back to the main point: Christians sin. Christians make mistakes. Christians are not perfect. Christians have not yet become all that God intends for them to be. However, there is a huge difference between being a sinner and being a hypocrite. A genuine Christian says, "Jesus Christ is my Savior but, yes, I have an ongoing issue of sin in my life that God is working to resolve." The hypocrite pretends to be something that he is not.

Christians have not yet become all that God intends for them to be.

To be fair, it is important to look at positive examples of Christians. Yes, there are counterfeits, but they are outnumbered hundreds to one by real Christians. I've been a Christian for years, and I have met thousands of other Christians. Overall I've been amazed by them. I have repeatedly seen people whose lives were terrible changed for good. I've seen people up against the most horrible situations, who have behaved in ways that I know they were not otherwise humanly capable of behaving. I have seen people who have been harshly treated who have literally and figuratively turned the other cheek and shown love to their enemies. I've seen it again and again. These are wonderful proofs of the validity of the difference that Jesus Christ makes in a person's life.

Hypocrites do not invalidate Jesus Christ. If he was who he claimed to be, then he is genuinely worthy of our faith whether there are hypocrites or not. Suppose you go to visit your physician. The doctor takes you into his office, sits you down, and says, "We need to have a very blunt conversation. There are two things you need to do. First, you need to lose forty pounds. Second, you need to quit smoking. If you don't do both, you are going to have severe illness and it will cost you your life." At first you are taken aback by the bluntness. But then you have something rolling through the back of your mind that bothers you. He's one hundred pounds overweight and has a pack of cigarettes in his pocket. You think to yourself, "Why should I lose weight? Why doesn't he lose a hundred pounds, and then we'll talk about it. Why doesn't he quit smoking, and then we'll discuss the subject. I'm not going to do it. So there!" In a more rational moment you might realize that the doctor's advice was good in spite of his hypocrisy.

Do not reject Jesus Christ because of the hypocrisy of some Christians.

So it is with the validity of the gospel of Jesus Christ. Don't reject the message because you don't like the messenger, and certainly do not reject Jesus Christ because of the hypocrisy of some Christians. In Matthew 23:13 Jesus was talking to the Pharisees, and he said to them, "Woe to you, teachers of the law and Pharisees, you hypocrites." This wasn't a private conversation. This was out in public. "Woe to you . . . you hypocrites. You shut the kingdom of heaven in men's faces. You yourselves do not enter, nor will you let those enter who are trying to." Jesus went on public record that these very religious Pharisees were hypocrites, and they weren't going to be allowed into the kingdom of God.

If you want another very interesting spin, consider Philippians 1:15–18. Here Paul is teaching about hypocrites, and he has a completely different angle. He's writing from prison in Rome, reflecting on what is happening with the young church and the growing but still small number of Christians. He says, "It is true that some preach Christ out of envy and rivalry, but others out of goodwill. The latter do so in love, knowing that I am put here [in prison] for the defense of the gospel. The former [the hypocrites] preach Christ out of selfish ambition, not sincerely, supposing that they can stir up trouble for me while I am in chains." So what does Paul think of this? He says, "But what does it matter? The important thing is that in every way, whether from false motives or true, Christ is preached."

Clearly Paul did not want them to have bad motives. He did not want them to be selfish. He did not want them to cause trouble for him. But he decided to look on the bright side and to rejoice every time the gospel of Jesus Christ was communicated, even if the people who were doing it were hypocrites, even if their motivations were wrong. In other words, he was able to distinguish the good message from the bad messengers.

No one should miss out on the gospel of Jesus Christ or on becoming a Christian because of hypocrites. Frankly, the hypocrites aren't worth it. They shouldn't be given that kind of credence and value.

PRACTICE WHAT WE PROFESS

As Christians it is extremely important that we practice what we profess. We do not want to be hypocrites. We need to realize that the Christian life is not a game; it is not something on a stage. It is important that we live consistently, matching up what we say we believe and the way we live.

The Bible is very straightforward about this in the book of James. James, you may recall, was a half brother of Jesus. He was concerned about people who say they have faith but don't act like it.

> What good is it, my brothers, if a man claims to have faith but has no deeds? Can such faith save him? Suppose a brother or

sister is without clothes and daily food. If one of you says to him, "Go, I wish you well; keep warm and well fed" but does nothing about his physical needs, what good is it? In the same way, faith by itself, if it is not accompanied by action, is dead.

But someone will say, "You have faith; I have deeds." Show me your faith without deeds, and I will show you my faith by what I do. You believe there is one God. Good! Even the demons believe that—and shudder. (James 2:14–19)

James is saying that if you want to make comparisons, look at the demons—the followers of Satan. They have pretty good theology. They believe in God, but they have evil behavior.

To be a Christian is to have behavior that is consistent with our beliefs. It is hypocrisy to say one thing and to do another thing. Please don't be a Christian and then turn around and mistreat other people. Don't claim to be a Christian and then have sex outside of marriage. Don't claim to be a Christian and then steal from an employer or cheat on an income tax return. Don't claim to be a Christian and then be selfish or greedy with money and other possessions.

To be a Christian is to submit to the lordship of Jesus Christ. In the first and second century there was a popular civil expression: "Caesar is Lord." The Christians picked up on that and changed one word. They wouldn't say, "Caesar is Lord"; they said, "Jesus is Lord." James was saying that it wasn't enough to just say the words; we need to live the way Jesus Christ wants us to live.

> *It is important for every Christian to recognize that our behavior impacts others.*

The primary reason for living Christianly is for the sake of God. However, it is also important for every Christian to recognize that our behavior impacts others. When I get to know people at Wooddale Church, I often ask, "How did you first come to Wooddale?" I've gotten some wonderful stories, but this was one of the most memorable.

A man told me that he was going through a difficult time in his life—he knew he needed something, but he didn't know exactly what he needed. He was working at a large multinational company based in the Twin Cities, and in his searching for answers he observed the lives of his co-workers. After many months of doing this, he concluded that four people stood out as different. He then sought opportunities to have private conversations with each of them and, as subtly as he could, asked them why they were the way they were. Each of those people said, "It is because I'm a Christian." Out of those conversations, he was invited to Wooddale Church, and he himself became a Christian with personal faith in Jesus Christ.

What impresses me is that for months those co-workers did not know they were being watched. He was looking at the way they dressed, the way they did their work, the way they dealt with difficulty, the vocabulary they used, what time they came to work, and what time they left. Everything about them. He was profoundly impressed by who they were, and they didn't even know that he was looking.

There's a story here for us all. Our lives greatly impact other people—our families, our neighbors, all the people that we work with. As Christians it is extremely important to be aware of the impact we have on other people, both positive and negative. For if our lives are not consistent with what we profess, if we live immorally and unbiblically, then our behavior impacts the lives of our children, of our employees, of our employer, our co-workers and friends, and even our enemies. May our prayer be that no one be turned away from Jesus Christ because of the sinful misbehavior of any of us who claim Jesus Christ as Savior.

One final word. If you have been distracted from Jesus Christ because of the hypocrisy of another, I assure you that while that other person may have disappointed you more than words can describe, Jesus Christ will never disappoint you.

CHAPTER TWENTY-TWO

JESUS AND SATAN

According to one survey, 45 percent of Americans don't believe in Satan. But Jesus did. Jesus believed in Satan because he saw him and talked to him. There's a fascinating account of their conversation in Matthew 4:1–11.

> Then Jesus was led by the Spirit into the desert to be tempted by the devil. After fasting forty days and forty nights, he was hungry. The tempter came to him and said, "If you are the Son of God, tell these stones to become bread."
>
> Jesus answered, "It is written: 'man does not live on bread alone, but on every word that comes from the mouth of God.'"
>
> Then the devil took him to the holy city and had him stand on the highest point of the temple. "If you are the Son of God," he said, "throw yourself down. For it is written: 'He will command his angels concerning you, and they will lift you up in their hands, so that you will not strike your foot against a stone.'"
>
> Jesus answered him, "It is also written: 'Do not put the Lord

your God to the test.'" Again, the devil took him to a very high mountain and showed him all the kingdoms of the world and their splendor. "All this I will give you," he said, "if you will bow down and worship me." Jesus said to him, "Away from me, Satan! For it is written: 'Worship the Lord your God, and serve him only.'"

Then the devil left him, and angels came and attended him.

The background for this historic conversation between Jesus and Satan is strange. Matthew says that Jesus was led by the Spirit into the desert to be tempted by the devil. "Tempted" may not be the best translation of the Greek word. Maybe it would be better to say, "tested." Either way, why would the Holy Spirit of God take Jesus into a desert for the stated purpose of being tempted or tested by the devil? Isn't that a strange thing to do?

Suppose a student graduates Phi Beta Kappa, valedictorian of the university graduating class. He or she goes on to law school and gets straight A's all the way through. Faculty members say that this is the best and the brightest student that they have ever had. Does that person still have to take the bar examination? Of course. Will he or she likely pass that examination? Of course. Even though everyone knows in advance that this student will do extraordinarily well, he or she still must take the test.

For thirty years Jesus received straight A's in everything he did. Everyone—God and humans alike—said there was never another like him. He was given the title Messiah. At his baptism a heavenly voice declared him to be God's beloved Son. Did he have to take a test before he could officially begin his public ministry as Messiah? Yes, he did. Was he likely to pass that test? Of course. But he still had to take it.

The Holy Spirit led him one day to a most unusual testing room, a wilderness area fifteen miles wide, thirty-five miles long, to the south and east of Jerusalem. It was a bleak, unpopulated desert—extremely rough terrain with a series of limestone formations and loose rocks everywhere. There Jesus waited for forty days and forty nights, praying and fasting in preparation for his big examination.

Then the examiner showed up. Satan had been preparing too, putting together the toughest test he could—because he was intent on making Jesus fail.

STONES OR BREAD

Satan started with test item number one. He said to Jesus, "If you are the Son of God, tell these stones to become bread." It isn't that he doubted Jesus was the Son of God, but rather he took advantage of Jesus' desperate hunger. He knew that Jesus was capable of miraculously turning the stones to bread and he wanted Jesus to do it.

Jesus understood that he faced some significant decisions. What appeared on the surface to be a simple test was really far more complex and complicated, just as our situations often are. Jesus had to decide before he answered how he was going to use his supernatural powers. Was he going to use them primarily for his comfort or for God's purposes? It is the same decision faced by every Christian who has wealth and power and influence. We must make a critical decision as to whether we will use them for our comfort and benefit or for the purposes of God.

It is tempting to sacrifice the future on the altar of the present.

Jesus had to decide whether he was going to take a short-term or a long-term perspective. Did he want what would be nice for now or what would be best for tomorrow? It is a decision that we often face. It is tempting to sacrifice the future on the altar of the present.

Jesus also had to decide how he was going to win the people whom he had set out in life to win. Was he going to win them by feeding them bread? If the word got out that he could turn the limestone into loaves of bread, hungry people from all over the ancient world would flock to this desert to eat. But he recalled that the people of Israel in a different desert at a different time had also been hungry and that God had sent down manna from heaven. While at first they were delighted to eat it, it wasn't too many hours before their delight turned to complaint.

As tempting as it must have been, Jesus decided not to do what Satan suggested. Even though it meant staying hungry, even though it meant being accused by Satan and others that he really couldn't do it, and even though it meant that Satan might use this against him, Jesus refused. He said to Satan, "It is written, man does not live on bread alone, but on every word that comes from the mouth of God." Jesus used the most potent weapon in his arsenal, the Word of God. He quoted Deuteronomy 8:3, where the ancient Hebrew people were in the desert griping about the manna God was feeding them. It was a reminder to them that feeding their stomachs was not the most important thing in life, that feasting on the Word of God had far greater value.

Jesus wasn't saying our physical needs are unimportant, but he was saying they aren't everything, and they are not most important. The greatest value in life is God, and what God says is more important than eating. Some people live for food. Other people live for sex. Others live for material possessions.

There is a powerful truth that can be documented outside of the Bible and Christian belief. It is the truth that people who devote their lives to feeding themselves or satisfying their sexual drive or accumulating material wealth do not find satisfaction therein. Those people come to the end of their lives only to be devastated by the disappointment that things are not as they had dreamed they would be. Some may say, "That might be true, but give me a ten-year try. Just give me lots to eat, unlimited sex, wealth, and power and let me find out for myself." That is a tragic and suicidal approach because the overwhelming testimony is that those who have done it have found themselves to be miserable.

Only God satisfies. That's a hard lesson for many of us to learn. Too many people wreck their lives finding it out. Many people will never believe it, but it is true.

That's why Jesus said what he said, and that's why Jesus passed his first test with an A+. He refused to use his power for himself. He refused to be a materialist, no matter how loudly his stomach grumbled. He insisted that God is the ultimate satisfier because "man does not live by bread alone, but on every word that comes from the mouth of God."

TESTING GOD

Jesus passed the first test. Satan was ready with the second. This time Satan said, "Jesus, if you are the Son of God, throw yourself down." For this test he took him on a field trip to the temple, the highest point in Jerusalem. Ancient records tell us it was 180 feet high. It was from there that Satan said, "Jump!"

Satan, who knows the Bible very well, tried Jesus' strategy with a quote from Psalm 91:11–12: "He will command his angels concerning you . . . they will lift you up in their hands, so that you will not strike your foot against a stone." It was absolutely true. Jesus could have jumped and he could have survived, just as he could have turned the rocks into loaves of bread. But Jesus also knew that there was far more to this test than surviving an eighteen-story plunge. He knew it was an invitation to win the loyalty of people through sensationalism. The courtyard below the temple pinnacle was the busiest and most visible place in Jerusalem. If people saw him jump and survive it, then they might follow him. In modern terminology you might say they would look up and say, "It's a bird, it's a plane; no, it's the Messiah!" and follow him. It must have been tempting to Jesus.

Jesus understood that crowds won by sensationalism are crowds seldom kept. Jesus decided not to jump, but again he quoted from the

Bible, this time from Deuteronomy 6:16. He told Satan, "It is also written: 'Do not put the Lord your God to the test.'"

But wait a minute, isn't that precisely what we are supposed to do? Aren't we supposed to test God and let everybody see how great he is? If we put something really tough in front of God and he comes through, then everybody is going to believe. Do you understand there is a big difference between testing God and trusting God? Trusting God is depending upon him to bring good from the circumstances of life into which he has led us, but testing God is manipulating the situation to get ourselves out of circumstances that we ought never to have been in.

For example, someone says, "I don't know if the Bible means it or not when it says a Christian shouldn't marry a non-Christian. I'm going to marry a non-Christian and just trust God to bring that person to faith in Jesus Christ." That's not trust, that's disobeying and testing God. Or somebody says, "I think I'll rob a bank. I'm going to do this right. I'll park the getaway car a block away, and before I get out I'm going to pray and commit the bank robbery to the Lord in every detail. I'm going to ask that God will intervene on my behalf and let me have a clean getaway. Who knows, I may even split 50/50 with God if the take is really good." That's not trusting God, that's testing God. How about the person who says, "I'm not going to study for the test because I can depend upon God to give me the answers." These people are not trusting God. They are putting God to the test, and he doesn't like it or allow it.

> *Trust is complete confidence and dependence upon God for the right outcome.*

Trusting God is relying on him to give us the strength to break off a relationship that we know is wrong. Trusting God is being faithful to him by not robbing the bank but counting upon him to provide our needs and have them met honestly. Trust is complete confidence and dependence upon God for the right outcome to the situation into which he has led us.

Jesus knew that the "temple jump-off" was an artificially contrived and manipulated test that Satan had made. It was not what God wanted, so Jesus refused to sinfully put God to the test.

WORSHIP ME

Satan then came up with his third and toughest test of all. He said, "Jesus, all this I give to you if you will bow down and worship me." He took Jesus to the top of the world so that he could look at all the kingdoms. He said, "Jesus, if you will worship me, it's yours for the taking." I think Jesus faced a very tough decision, because this time it wasn't for him, it was for us.

The thought must have run through Jesus' mind that Satan has ruined the world. There are wars, diseases, disharmony, violence, ugliness, crime, and sin. If Jesus ruled the world, it would suddenly be different. There wouldn't be all of the horrible consequences upon humans. He could skip the Messianic journey and bypass the Crucifixion. He could just go right to the results without going through all the pain. He could do something great and good immediately.

I am reminded of the year that our country entered into war in the Persian Gulf. Suppose Saddam Hussein of Iraq had taken the Emir of Kuwait on a plane ride above the country of Kuwait and had said to him, "It's yours; you can have it all: the oil wells, the gold, the ships, the airplanes, everything. It's yours if you will simply bow down and worship me." If such a thing had happened, the Emir of Kuwait might have thought that then there would be no war—no rapes, no suffering, or death, or devastation. But then, I hope, he would have answered, "You can't give it to me, it *is* mine. You stole it! Besides, Saddam, you can't be trusted!"

That is essentially what Jesus responded to Satan. "Satan, it's not yours to give. It's mine. I am the King of Kings and the Lord of Lords. What's more, Satan, I don't trust you." So Jesus said no. He chose to do it the right way, even though it was the hard way. "Away from me, Satan! For it is written, 'Worship the Lord your God, and serve him only.'"

The greatest good in life is to live for and to worship God. Nothing is worth the ultimate sin of taking from God his rightful worship and giving it to Satan.

The story ends with Satan leaving and Jesus exhausted, and the angels coming to attend him. A couple of years ago, when we were in Asia, I learned something that touched me deeply about the perspective of our fellow Christians in the People's Republic of China. They said their experience was that if you are truly a disciple of Jesus Christ you will suffer, because suffering is an essential part of what being a Christian is all about. But they also said that suffering will always be followed by God's great relief and blessing. That's the way it was for Jesus.

As we leave the conversation between Jesus and Satan, the lesson seems obvious. We too will be tested by the Enemy. We know that. The tests will not be easy. We will be tempted to sin. The answer is to follow the example of Jesus—to say *no* to Satan, to make Scripture our weapon, and to remain faithful to God—no matter what.

CHAPTER TWENTY-THREE

POSSESSED

I suppose it is safe to say that we in America today, more than at any other time or place in all of history, count possessions as among life's most important relationships. It is an issue where Christians have gone to great extremes. There are those on the one hand who emphasize poverty. They quote Jesus as saying we should sell all that we have and give to the poor. And then there are those who emphasize prosperity. They teach that God is a rich God and we are his children. Therefore, he intends for us to be as healthy and wealthy as we possibly can. On the one extreme we are made to feel guilty if we have any possessions at all. On the other extreme we are made to feel cheated if we are not billionaires or if we don't have more than everyone else.

Since possessions are such an important part of our American lives and since possessions were so much a part of the teaching of Jesus, let's try to figure out what is a truly Christian relationship to the things we own.

The Things We Own

Let's consider four biblical principles. The first and great overarching principle of all material possessions is that God made everything, God owns everything, and everything good that we have comes from God. In James 1:17 we read: "Every good and perfect gift is from above, coming down from the Father of the heavenly lights, who does not change like shifting shadows."

Everything that we have is owned by God. It is on loan to us— house, car, computer, books, and clothes. But he's very generous with all that he has. So God has allowed us to live in his world, drive his cars, eat his food, enjoy his art, wear his clothes, and occupy his houses. God loves doing this. He loves to share all that is good.

Never make the mistake of thinking that we own what's really on loan to us. For the moment we make that mental mistake, we become thieves and are taking ownership of something that is not rightly ours.

The second principle to consider as Christians in our relationship to possessions is that we are to be grateful and enjoy God's generosity. I sometimes wonder why I was born in affluent America, where it is comparatively easy to get possessions, while others are born in places where there is not very much to be had even if they work very hard.

For me, it is a matter of trust. I believe that God is wise, kind, good, and just. When I put all that I know about God together with my observations of inequities in our world, I conclude that God knows answers that I have not been told. I anticipate that someday in eternity I will be told things that now I could not begin to understand. Until then I must trust God for that which I do not know, and I must behave Christianly on the basis of the information that I do have.

The Bible teaches gratitude and enjoyment. One example is in Ecclesiastes 5:19, where we read, "When God gives any man wealth and possessions, and enables him to enjoy them, to accept his lot and to be happy in his work—this is a gift of God."

In other words, God invites us to enjoy the many gifts he has given us.

Like God, I too am a father. And as a father I take delight in giving gifts to my children, and I want them to enjoy those gifts. I don't want them to feel guilty that they have something others don't have. I want my children to appreciate the gifts, to use the gifts, and to enjoy the gifts.

As Christians we need to count all the gifts that God has given to us. We ought to thank God for what he has given, and we ought to thoroughly enjoy every one.

The third principle for our relationship to possessions is that we are to enjoy wealth, but never to trust it. The day that our confidence is in the gifts that we have is the day that we have turned our backs on God. In 1 Timothy 6:17 the apostle Paul tells Timothy to "command those who are rich in this present world not to be arrogant nor to put their hope in wealth, which is so uncertain, but to put their hope in God, who richly provides us with everything for our enjoyment."

It doesn't take a lot of money to trust in money. You can take a nickel and hold it in front of your eye and blot out the entire sun. It doesn't take much more than a nickel's worth of wealth to block out God. It is switching our trust from God, who deserves our trust, and putting our trust in the gifts and the possessions he has given us.

Never trust money. Never trust possessions. Only trust God. At the very most, money and possessions are instruments God uses as means for good in our lives. Trust only the Giver.

The fourth principle for a Christian's relationship to possessions is to share God's blessings. In 1 Timothy 6:18–19 we find another command to those who are rich:

Command them to do good, to be rich in good deeds, and to

be generous and willing to share. In this way, they will lay up treasure for themselves as a firm foundation for the coming age, so that they may take hold of the life that is truly life.

The principle is simple and straightforward. Those who receive God's gifts should share those gifts with others.

I've been helped by the perspective of Dr. Ralph Winter, who is a church historian and theologian. He has a great and insightful analysis of the nation of Israel in the Old Testament. The people of Israel wanted to be blessed by God, but they didn't want to bless anybody else. They wanted God to bless them in a big way, but they were unwilling to share those blessings with others. As a result, eventually God quit blessing them.

The same principle is repeated in the New Testament as well as in our times. The New Testament tells us that it is more blessed to give than to receive. The only way to keep God's blessings is to give them away. The only way to get new blessings from God is to share the old ones and make room for more.

AN ABUNDANCE OF POSSESSIONS

Perhaps we could say that covetousness is the opposite of generosity. Give sufficient attention to Jesus' words when he says, "Take heed, and beware of all covetousness; for a man's life does not consist in the abundance of his possessions" (Luke 12:15 RSV). That's a big message from the mouth of the master. He wants it clearly understood, so he illustrates with a three-point parable.

> And he told them this parable: "The ground of a certain rich man produced a good crop. He thought to himself, 'What shall I do? I have no place to store my crops.'
> "Then he said, 'This is what I'll do. I will tear down my barns and build bigger ones, and there I will store all my grain and my

goods. And I'll say to myself, "You have plenty of good things laid up for many years. Take life easy; eat, drink and be merry." '

"But God said to him, 'You fool! This very night your life will be demanded from you. Then who will get what you have prepared for yourself?'

"This is how it will be with anyone who stores up things for himself but is not rich toward God." (Luke 12:16–21)

Point number one is success: "The land of a rich man brought forth plentifully." This is the story of a man who had it made! He was rich and successful.

We've all fantasized about winning a tax-free million dollars, receiving an unexpected inheritance, or winning a lawsuit. We'd love to experience such success. Yet seldom do we think about the downside. Are the happiest people you know also the richest people you know? Seldom when we imagine that type of success for ourselves or for anyone else do we think about how riches often lead not to contentment but to tragedy.

When we read Jesus' words in Mark 10:25, "It is easier for a camel to go through the eye of a needle than it is for a rich man to enter the kingdom of God," we often spend more energy explaining the meaning of the "eye of the needle" (a gate in the city of Jerusalem) than considering the warning of the danger of riches.

Success and riches can be your greatest enemy.

And so Jesus says to me, "Take heed, and beware of all covetousness; for a man's life does not consist in the abundance of his possessions." The Greek word that's translated as *beware* literally means *to take positive action to ward off a foe.* The idea is that we're being attacked and we've got to immediately do something significant to fight against the tremendous foe that's out to get us. Jesus is saying to me and to you, "Watch out for the stuff called success. Watch out for it, and take positive action to ward off the dangers, because success and riches—and particularly the desire for more riches—can be your greatest enemy."

The second point in Jesus' parable is about self. Listen to the thoughts of the farmer in verses 17–19:

> He thought to himself, "What shall I do? I have no place to store my crops." Then he said, "This is what I'll do. I will tear down my barns and build bigger ones, and there I will store all my grain and my goods. And I'll say to myself, 'You have plenty of good things laid up for many years. Take life easy; eat, drink and be merry.' "

Several positive things can be said about this farmer. He was a good business manager. He used his resources well. He was a man of vision, decision, and the kind of person who planned ahead. He made provision possible for the lean years ahead. In one sense he was consistent with what Jesus taught in other parables about money. He didn't hoard his money but used it for ease, food, and pleasure. He took what he had and did something with it.

So why did he get into so much trouble? The problem here is "self." He was completely selfish. He frequently used the personal pronouns "I" and "my."

This man did not consider himself a steward of what God lent to him. He really believed that everything he had was his. He thought his security for the future was in his possessions. He was a fool! He figured the more money he had the longer he would live.

He wasn't alone, for this is a timeless phenomenon. Who is really more prone to trust God, the rich or the poor? When you reflect back on your own experience as I often have, is it not adversity that tends to draw us to God far more than prosperity? There may be some exceptions, but don't write your rule by the exception. It is most often the tough experiences of life that cause us to come close to the Lord, and it is the prosperous experiences of life that tend to cause us to trust in ourselves.

When we pray for our daily bread in the Lord's Prayer, it may be little more than a ritual, because we have plenty of food. We live in homes where the refrigerator is full. When we have money in our pockets, we don't particularly trust God for "daily bread." When we live in comfortable homes we're not likely to pray for a place to sleep. Only if that comfortable home is lost do we then in that adversity turn to God and depend upon him. When we have comprehensive health insurance we don't worry about paying our medical bills. It is what we *don't* have that tends to draw us closest to God.

There's an old Roman proverb that says that money is like seawater. The more a man drinks the thirstier he becomes.

Does all this mean that money is bad? No, but it is dangerous. God says to the farmer, "Fool! This night your soul is required of you; and the things you have prepared, whose will they be?"

The farmer was so sure he was secure. He thought he had everything under control. But he didn't. God decides the ultimate issue: death. The farmer indeed was a fool. He had made a success of everything except what mattered most.

Our society screams the importance of success and self. Pick up today's newspaper or turn to any TV station and you can't escape the message that success, money, and possessions bring power and make life good. But it's wrong.

Jesus tells us the real truth: "This is how it will be with anyone who lays up treasure for himself but is not rich toward God." The alternative is to be rich toward God. J. B. Phillips paraphrases this verse as "rich where God is concerned."

This is not suggesting that we have a bank account of good works in heaven where God keeps some sort of celestial computer record. It is talking about where we put our trust and our confidence. When our trust and confidence is in God and not in money or possessions then we are rich toward him. And only then do we really see possessions as a means and not an end. They are to be used primarily for God's glory rather than for our glory.

The practical test for this is to imagine losing all of one's possessions. Ask yourself, "What if I lost everything?" What would that do to you? Would it ruin your life? Would it be such a disaster that you can't imagine how you could go on? That's an indication that you have the wrong priorities. On the other hand, if your response would be, "Losing everything would be a terrible inconvenience and not the way I would ever choose it to be, but I still have my Lord and I still trust God even if everything else is gone," then you are "rich toward God." Your priorities are right.

I still have my Lord and I still trust God even if everything else is gone.

William Barclay tells the story about a conversation between an ambitious young man and an older wiser friend.

Young man: "I will learn my trade."
Older man: "And then?"
Young man: "I will set up my business."
Older man: "And then?"
Young man: "I will make my fortune."
Older man: "And then?"
Young man: "Well, I suppose that I will grow old and retire and enjoy my money."
Older man: "And then?"
Young man: "Well, I suppose that someday I'll die."
Older man: "And then?"[1]

What about you? What are you really living for? Jesus said, "Take

[1]William Barclay, *The Gospel of Luke* (Philadelphia: The Westminster Press, 1975), 165.

heed, and beware of all covetousness; for a man's life does not consist in the abundance of his possessions."

We need to renounce success and self as our priorities and claim Jesus and riches toward God as our new priorities. To have a Christian relationship with possessions, remember that everything good comes from God. Be grateful and enjoy God's generosity. Never trust wealth. Share God's blessings. As we are blessed, let us bless others. In that way we will deepen our friendship with God.

CHAPTER TWENTY-FOUR

THE WAY TO HEAVEN

It is often a turnoff to inquirers of Christianity when Christians insist that Jesus Christ is the only way to heaven. It seems like Christians so often are intent on pushing Christian ideas without a genuine consideration of the other person's interests, beliefs, or needs. Christians can seem to be guilty of the worst of religious arrogance. What right do Christians have to say that Christians are right and everybody else is wrong? What about Buddhists, Hindus, Muslims, Jews, animists, pantheists, Satanists, pagans, and atheists? Does not each person have a right to believe whatever he or she chooses to believe? Isn't one religion as good as another as long as a person is sincere in the beliefs that he or she holds?

The commonsense approach of our culture repeatedly tells us that there are lots of ways to accomplish the same thing: "All roads lead to Rome"; "There's more than one way to skin a cat"; "All religions are different ways to the same God."

Whether a person chooses to be a Christian or chooses some other faith is entirely up to that individual. It is a matter of private and personal choice. However, it seems good to at least understand Christianity by hearing what Jesus Christ and his followers had to say in the Bible.

THE ONLY ONE

In John 14:6 Jesus is involved in a conversation. He said, "I am the way and the truth and the life. No one comes to the Father except through me." Notice that Jesus did not say, "I am *a* way or *a* truth or I am *a* means to get to the Father." He's absolutely exclusive in his claim that he is the only one who can provide a personal relationship with God. You might read that and think he was using hyperbole. Maybe he was overstating the case and there could be other interpretations of that quote from Jesus.

But let's look at another quote from Jesus, this one in John 8:24. Once again, he is very pointed in explaining: "I told you that you would die in your sins; if you do not believe that I am the one I claim to be, you will indeed die in your sins." That statement, along with the whole conversation surrounding it in John 8, was so offensive to the religious people who were listening to Jesus that by the end of the conversation they picked up rocks and were going to stone him. They were going to kill him because he was insisting that he was the only way to get to God.

This same teaching was picked up by Jesus' followers. In Acts 4:12 Peter is speaking to religious leaders in the city of Jerusalem. He tells them, "Salvation is found in no one else, for there is no other name under heaven given to men by which we must be saved." It's hard to mistake the point that is being made. He's declaring that without faith in the person and the name of Jesus Christ, there is no other way to be saved from sin and to have eternal life in heaven. Jesus is the only way.

What Peter said in Acts 4:12, Paul echoes in 1 Timothy 2:5. In the previous verse Paul teaches that God wants everyone to be saved from sin and to come to the knowledge of truth. He goes on to explain how a person gets salvation and learns the truth about God. He says, "There is one God and one mediator between God and men, the man Christ Jesus." It's another one of these all-or-nothing statements. There's only one way to God. It's not through saints, it's not through some other religion, and it's not through doing good deeds. The only way to God is through Jesus Christ. He is it. It's all or nothing.

If I were an objector to Christianity and I read these statements, maybe they would drive me away more than they would draw me close. However, these lines from the Bible would be helpful to me in understanding why Christians say what they say. For often Christians are perceived as arrogant and presumptuous

The only way to God is through Jesus Christ. It's all or nothing.

in their claim that "because I'm a Christian I'm going to heaven and other people are not going to heaven because they are not Christians." These verses would help me to understand that Christians aren't claiming to be smarter and superior to everyone else. They are just saying that this is what the Bible teaches. This is what Jesus said. This is God's plan and not ours.

The Bible teaches that all humans are sinners who are alienated from God; therefore we are excluded from heaven. God is holy; he cannot tolerate sin. Nothing that we can do will work to remedy our situation. So unless God steps in and does something, we're done. But God did step in.

NO OTHER WAY

Recall from part 1 of this book how we can know God: God's solution to our alienation is Jesus Christ, his Son. He sent his Son from heaven to earth. For thirty-three years Jesus lived a perfect life that qualified him to be a substitute who could take the sin of other people. He was then sent to a cross to die. He took all the human sin of all of history on himself, and he paid the penalty for sin when he died on the cross and then rose back to life again.

Couldn't God have done it some other way? If he's God, why couldn't he just say, "Poof! All sin is forgiven!" Why not just pardon everybody? Or why doesn't he set up a system of credits and debits so that if you do bad stuff you get a debit and if you do good stuff you get a credit, and by the day you die you hope to be at least one ahead on the credits? Then it would be up to everybody to sort of work it out for themselves. Or why didn't God endorse all the different religions that people come up with and say that they all lead to heaven? Wouldn't that be a better alternative than killing his own Son?

Seriously, would God send his Son to die if there was any other way of doing it? Now, if you're a parent, think about that. Would you give your own child to be sacrificed if there was any other way of accomplishing whatever you were trying to accomplish? It seems obvious that God sent Jesus to die because that was the only solution. That was the only thing that would work. There simply was no other way.

There simply was no other way.

Think of the one person whom you love more than anyone else in the world. Now, as horrible as the thought is, imagine that person suffering severe injuries in a terrible accident that has left him on life support in a hospital. As you stand by the bed, the attending physician comes in and says that this person whom you love so very much is brain dead and there's no point in continuing life support. He asks if you would be willing to sign a consent form so that his organs could be donated to help other people live. The physician says, "Why don't you take an hour and a half to think about it, and I'll meet you back here."

You put the form in your pocket and start walking down the hall in a daze. As you wander through the hospital something happens that is never supposed to happen. Through a series of events you find out who the intended recipient of your loved one's heart is supposed to be. This person is going to die very soon without a heart transplant. It is her only hope. And so, in one of the most difficult decisions you've ever made, you take the pen and sign the consent form. Shortly thereafter, the one you love is taken from life support and his heart is removed. And then to your absolute amazement you find out that at the very last moment the intended recipient refuses the heart. It is too late to find another compatible recipient, and the heart is going to go to waste.

You are so dumbfounded that you rush to the room of the intended recipient and demand, "Why?" The intended recipient turns to you and says, "There are a lot of different ways to deal with heart disease. I've decided from now on I'm going to take an aspirin every day, become a vegetarian, and start running a few miles a day. And I was reading this article about some alternative medicine you can buy over the counter in Tijuana, Mexico, and so probably later this week I'm going to travel to Mexico and buy this medicine and start taking it."

Your mouth hangs open in amazement. You don't know whether you feel pity or rage. You blurt out the words, "Are you crazy? None of that stuff will work! You're past taking an aspirin every day. Eating a few carrots is not going to change your situation. None of these things will save your life. You are signing your own death certificate. Your only hope is the transplanted heart from the person I love more than anyone else in the world."

God's plan to save our souls for eternity is absolutely brilliant. It was completely sacrificial but, most of all, it's the only way that would work. Nothing else would work and so that's why he did it.

SINCERITY ISN'T ENOUGH

The objector insists, "There have got to be some other ways to heaven! As long as I sincerely believe, God certainly will accept that as enough."

Does it really make sense that all roads lead to heaven as long as you're sincere? It's hard to find an example of that principle working in any area of life. If you have high blood pressure or if you have glaucoma or diabetes, you must take the right medicine for whatever the malady is. You can't just take any medicine because you're sincere. If in the middle of the night you wake up with a headache and you mistakenly grab the rat poison instead of the Tylenol, do you think you're going to wake up tomorrow morning healthy and headache-free just because you were sincere?

Not that sincerity isn't good. It's very important. But sincerity does not make the wrong way into the right way any more than sincerity makes a wrong religion right.

To claim that all religions lead to heaven is both naïve and ignorant. It's the type of statement made by someone who probably isn't very knowledgeable about religion. The truth is that most religions of the world are contradictory one to the other.

For example, Christianity teaches the deity, death, and resurrection of Jesus Christ. Islam denies the deity, the death, and the resurrection of Jesus Christ. Hinduism says there are thousands of gods. Christianity says there is only one God. Christianity says that Jesus is God and that he is the Messiah. Judaism insists that Jesus is not God and he is not the Messiah. These opposing teachings cannot all be true at the same time. Some are right and some are wrong.

It is more intellectually honest to say that Christianity is wrong and some other religion is right than to insist that contradictory religions are all right and that they all lead to God and heaven. That just doesn't make sense.

For those who insist there is a better way to God than the way of Christianity, I encourage them to do all they can to pursue it. But I'd like to offer some guidelines to consider.

First, at least give Christianity a full and a fair chance. Let Christianity compete in the search for a true religion. Read the Bible—don't base your judgment on what somebody else has said about it. Read the Bible in its entirety. Be bold enough to say, "God, if you are there, if this is the true way, please show me. And if you'll help me to believe, then I will."

A second guideline is to beware of the danger of searching forever. There are hundreds, perhaps thousands of different religions in the world, and because the major religions are so complex it would take more than a lifetime to check them all out. A different approach must be taken. If you have an undiagnosed illness, you go from doctor to doctor until

Be bold enough to say, "God, if you are there, if this is the true way, please show me."

you find someone who figures out what is the matter and what should be done to remedy it. When that happens, you stop your search. You don't have to see every doctor in the world; you only search until you find one who can help you. The same approach can be taken with religion. It's not a matter of examining every religious claim of truth—instead, determine to limit the search to finding the one that works. When you find one that will meet your needs, the search will end.

A third guideline before making your final choice is to compare the religion you are considering to Jesus Christ. I believe those who do, discover that Jesus and the Bible compare favorably to every potential competitor. I'm convinced that Jesus Christ, when put head to head in comparison with any other religion, will invariably prove to be superior and will be the only true faith.

Author and speaker Josh McDowell offers a fascinating challenge: "Suppose a group of us are taking a hike in a very dense forest. As we get deeper into the forest we become lost. Realizing that taking the wrong path now might mean that we will lose our lives, we begin to be afraid. However, we soon notice that ahead in the distance, where the trail splits, there are two human forms at the fork in the road. Running up to these people, we notice that one has on a park ranger uniform, and he is standing there perfectly healthy and alive, while the other person is lying face down, dead. Now which of these two are we going to ask about the way out? Obviously, the one who is living.

"When it comes to eternal matters we are going to ask the one who is alive the way out of the predicament. This is not Mohammed. Not Confucius, but Jesus Christ. Jesus is unique. He came back from the dead. This demonstrates that He is the one whom He claimed to be, the unique Son of God and the only way by which a person can have a personal relationship with the true and living God."[1]

God of heaven and earth, I pray for those who are seeking for you that they will not be disappointed. May they discover the reality that you are the true Seeker—far more than any of us. You are the one who sent your Son to die for the sins of each of us, and you have been seeking us ever since. I pray that you will chase the doubts away. I pray that you will give faith. I pray that you will turn doubters into believers and answer the objections. I pray that they'll become Christians through Jesus Christ. Amen.

---

[1]Josh McDowell, *Answers to Tough Questions Skeptics Ask About the Christian Faith* (San Bernardino, Calif.: Here's Life Publishers, Inc., 1980), 63–64.

CHAPTER TWENTY-FIVE

THE WAY TO HELL

Many say that they cannot believe what the Bible says and become a Christian because it is impossible for them to accept that a good God would send people to hell. What kind of God would take pleasure in the eternal suffering of human beings? Why would God not automatically use his power and bring everybody to heaven? Or at the very least, why doesn't God annihilate hell and everybody that's in it to put an end to their suffering? Besides, even the idea of heaven seems tarnished by the thought that the perfection and happiness there must be lessened by the realization of millions of others suffering in hell.

Frankly, hell is a most unpleasant subject, and because of that it is a topic upon which you will rarely hear a sermon or a serious discussion. It is sometimes something of an embarrassment to theologians. Generally we prefer to emphasize that which is positive rather than negative. However, if Christians are to be open and honest, then no topic is off limits, no matter how hard it is. We need to tackle the topic of hell and whether God would send people there.

What the Bible Says

Here is what the Bible teaches. In John 3:36, Jesus said, "Whoever believes in the Son has eternal life, but whoever rejects the Son will not see life, for God's wrath remains on him."

In John 5:28–29: "Do not be amazed at this, for a time is coming when all who are in their graves will hear his voice and come out— those who have done good will rise to live, and those who have done evil will rise to be condemned."

In Matthew 10:28, he said, "Do not be afraid of those who kill the body but cannot kill the soul. Rather, be afraid of the One who can destroy both soul and body in hell."

Matthew 5:22 is where Jesus spoke about the "danger of the fire of hell," and in Mark 9:43, he warned of the consequence of hell, "where the fire never goes out."

In Luke 16:23–24, Jesus tells the story about a rich man who died, was buried, and went to hell, where he was in "torment" and pleaded for someone to come and to "dip the tip of his finger in water and cool my tongue, because I am in agony in this fire."

Second Peter 2:4 tells us that "God did not spare angels when they sinned, but sent them to hell, putting them into gloomy dungeons to be held for judgment."

Jude 13 refers to the "blackest darkness that has been reserved forever."

At the end of the Bible, in Revelation 20:11–15, John reports a preview of the future:

> Then I saw a great white throne and him who was seated on it. Earth and sky fled from his presence, and there was no place for them. And I saw the dead, great and small, standing before the throne, and books were opened. Another book was opened, which is the book of life. The dead were judged according to what they had done as recorded in the books. The sea gave up

the dead that were in it, and death and Hades gave up the dead that were in them, and each person was judged according to what he had done. Then death and Hades were thrown into the lake of fire. The lake of fire is the second death. If anyone's name was not found written in the book of life, he was thrown into the lake of fire.

The conclusions that can be drawn from these passages are pretty straightforward. The first is that the Bible clearly teaches hell exists. Jesus, for all of his talk about love and goodness and forgiveness and heaven, is the same Jesus who talked about people going to hell. There should be no doubt that the Bible teaches hell exists or that Jesus believed in the existence of hell.

The second conclusion is that we don't know a lot of details. The language of the Bible communicates that hell is a terrible and a miserable place for evil people, but we don't know exactly what

> *There should be no doubt that the Bible teaches hell exists.*

it is like. The words used to describe hell in the Bible are metaphors—comparisons to our everyday vocabulary and experience. The Bible uses symbolic rather than literal descriptions.

For example, Matthew 5:22 refers to the "fire of hell," but Jude 13 speaks of the "blackest darkness" of hell. In our experience, where there is fire, there is light, and where there is blackest darkness, there is no light. Both are figures of speech to describe something that is awful. The point of the Bible is not that we imagine literal darkness, a bottomless pit, or a lake of fire. The point of the Bible is that hell is more awful than the combination of the worst words that we have in our vocabulary.

A third conclusion is that hell, in its definition and in its essence, is separation from God. Hell is a bad place. Hell is awful. Our word *hell* comes from the Hebrew word *Gehenna*. Gehenna actually is a place in the valley of Hinnom just south of the city of Jerusalem. In ancient times, before the Hebrew people took over Jerusalem and Palestine, it was the location of the altar to the god Molech, where pagan people sacrificed their own children. That was a most abominable practice to Jews. Perhaps that was in part why in later centuries Gehenna, or the valley of Hinnom, was where Jerusalem's garbage was dumped and burned. The constant flames and smoke made it an ugly, uninviting, smelly, terrible place. For the Hebrew people it was about as far distant as they could imagine from the temple in Jerusalem but even farther from God.

No one was suggesting that bad people were literally put in that particular garbage dump; rather it was understood that after death eternity was to be spent by sinners in a place that was as bad and godless as any place could possibly be. And they called that place *Gehenna.*

The existence of hell may not be the most important concern. Our primary concern is who goes to hell and how they get there.

Created to Be God's Friends

Certainly God does not want us to go to hell. There is never a hint in the Bible that God takes any pleasure in that kind of destiny for any person. Rather, the picture painted in the Bible is of a God who not only hates sin but who also hates hell. In 2 Peter 3:9, we are explicitly told that God does not want anyone to perish but wants everyone to repent and to go to heaven.

God initially created us all to be his friends and to be his followers, and God's love for us is repeatedly declared in the Bible. We are described as his children. We are to call him Father. Like any good father, he desires the very best for those who are his sons and daughters; he certainly does not want anything bad to happen to any of his children.

But while that is true, it is also true that there are aspects of God's character that require there to be a hell. Remember that God is a holy

God. He has nothing to do with sin; he is distant from it; he can't be around it. Therefore, there must be an alternative to heaven for those who insist on holding on to their sin. Initially hell was to be the destination of Satan and the other defectors from heaven who did not want to follow God (Matthew 25:41). Hell is the opposite of heaven—the alternative destination.

Recall, too, that when God created us to be his friends and his followers, he also created us to make choices. He did not design us to be robots that are programmed to love him and to be controlled in every detail by his prior design. God gave us the choice to love him or to hate him, to be good or evil. That choice necessitates hell. Otherwise, God would have to impose his will upon all of us. He would have to *make* us love him, *make* us choose what is right, and *make* us go to heaven,

It bears repeating: Never let it be thought that God wants *anyone* in hell. It is the exact opposite of God's intent and design and best for us. In order to avoid hell, he sent his one and only Son. He made the ultimate intervention, paid the ultimate price, gave the ultimate sacrifice.

It is a mistake to start with hell and then surmise what God is like. It is far better to begin with the clear character of God as presented in the Bible. The Bible is explicit in telling us that God is good. He is kind. He is loving. He is just. Whatever he does, it will be right, because that's who God is.

> *Never let it be thought that God wants* anyone *in hell.*

When these pieces are puzzled together, it leads us to the conclusion that hell is essentially a human choice. Not a choice in that someone sits down and says, "Well, I suppose I've got to choose between heaven and hell, and I would rather suffer in torment than go to heaven and be forever in bliss." Of course not. In fact, heaven and hell are not the central elements of the choice. The central elements are whether we choose God and good or whether we choose sin and evil. It is out of these primary choices that the consequences then flow.

THE CHOICE BETWEEN GOD AND SIN

Romans 1:20–32 speaks about God giving people over to sin:

> For since the creation of the world God's invisible qualities— his eternal power and divine nature—have been clearly seen, being understood from what has been made, so that men are without excuse.
>
> For although they knew God, they neither glorified him as God nor gave thanks to him, but their thinking became futile and their foolish hearts were darkened. Although they claimed to be wise, they became fools and exchanged the glory of the immortal God for images made to look like mortal man and birds and animals and reptiles.
>
> Therefore God gave them over in the sinful desires of their hearts to sexual impurity for the degrading of their bodies with one another. They exchanged the truth of God for a lie, and worshiped and served created things rather than the Creator—who is forever praised. Amen.
>
> Because of this, God gave them over to shameful lusts. Even their women exchanged natural relations for unnatural ones. In the same way the men also abandoned natural relations with women and were inflamed with lust for one another. Men committed indecent acts with other men, and received in themselves the due penalty for their perversion.
>
> Furthermore, since they did not think it worthwhile to retain the knowledge of God, he gave them over to a depraved mind, to do what ought not to be done. They have become filled with every kind of wickedness, evil, greed and depravity. They are full of envy, murder, strife, deceit and malice. They are gossips, slan-

derers, God-haters, insolent, arrogant and boastful; they invent ways of doing evil; they disobey their parents; they are senseless, faithless, heartless, ruthless. Although they know God's righteous decree that those who do such things deserve death, they not only continue to do these very things but also approve of those who practice them.

Repeated throughout this long section is the explanation that "God gave them over." Another way of saying it is that God let people go the way they insisted on going. God allows people to make their choices, even if he hates the consequences of those choices.

It happens all the time in daily life. Men and women drink, gamble, do drugs, or work excessive hours, until they have alienated their families. The problem gets greater and greater, until a husband or wife or others try to intervene and offer the person a choice: "You're going to have to choose between your addictive behavior and your family. You're going to lose everything if you continue down this path." Many choose to continue their bad behavior, even at the price of losing a spouse, children, house, job, everything. You might wonder why anyone would ever do that. Why would you give up what is good and even best for that which is not good and even the worst? Somehow our choices blind us to terrible consequences, and we continue no matter what.

God let people go the way they insisted on going.

That is what sin does to our human relationship with God. People go further and further down the path until they would rather hold on to the sin and go to hell than give up the sin, turn to God, and go to heaven. God allows bad choices to be made. God "lets them go" or "gives them over" to the direction they have freely chosen.

You may say, "All right, that makes some measure of sense. But take someone who has made awful choices repeatedly through forty, fifty, or even ninety years of life; I have trouble with saying the consequences for that comparatively short series of bad choices (considering eternity) must last forever and ever. Isn't that extreme?"

Have you ever considered the possibility that the permanence of hell may be more the choice of those who are on the inside than of God who is on the outside? Perhaps the path chosen in this life grows stronger rather than weaker in the next life. It was the great English writer C. S. Lewis who observed that the door of hell is locked tightly, but if you look closely it's locked from the inside not from the outside. In other words, the patterns set on earth continue to grow stronger and stronger after death. The choice against God becomes more and more adamant.

If all of this is so, it is not God that sends people to hell. It would be better to say that people send themselves to hell.

Does that answer all of the questions? Of course not. God is complex and the issues of eternity are complex. We are attempting to understand things that reach far beyond our usual ability to see and to understand. A few years ago the Hubbell telescope made it possible to see a star in our own galaxy that had never before been discovered. It is twelve million times the size of our sun. It is big enough to fill the entire space of the orbit of the earth around our sun. How did we miss something so big for so long? Space dust. According to astronomers, it has been shrouded from our sight by dust, and now through this super-powerful telescope it is possible to see what has been there all along.

This is no doubt true with regard to how we see God. God is bigger and brighter and more complicated than this superstar. From our human and earthly perspective, many things about God and his truth are clouded in the dust of our lives that blocks his brightness and his magnitude. We see only partially now and we have to trust for the rest. We may not feel comfortable with that, but it is the choice we must make. It is not only a Christian principle of faith but also an everyday principle for how we understand other things. There are and always will be unanswered questions.

Is it possible for persons to be saved from hell without Jesus Christ? No, it's not. At least not if you agree with what the Bible says. Is it possible that the blood of Jesus Christ and his sacrifice on the cross could save people from hell who may not fully understand all that it means to become a Christian? Yes, there were people in the Old Testament who were given eternal life through Jesus Christ although they predated him and did not know his name. They only had a promise of what God would provide. Yes, there are children who die in infancy, or those who are mentally disabled, and we believe that the blood of Jesus Christ will cover them. We believe that God will not do anything that is unfair or wrong.

Is it possible that someday God will decide to obliterate hell and annihilate all those who are there? Actually, some Bible-believing Christians would say yes, although most believe that such a thought is not consistent with a correct understanding of the significant teachings of the Bible.

We probably should not linger on what we don't know, but rather on what we do know. We know that every person who accepts Jesus Christ as Savior and Lord need never worry about hell again. Jesus Christ guarantees us eternal life in heaven—without a doubt.

Those who know the gospel's message but have never made a decision about it are the most accountable of all. How do you answer to a God who gave his Son, and say, "I was too busy to decide what to do"? We dare not reject God's offer of forgiveness of sin and eternal life and then somehow expect that God will open the gates of heaven and welcome us in.

As Christians let us take every opportunity to tell others. Remember, we have the very best news, and it really is true. It does matter that others know it and have an opportunity to change their eternal destiny.

We know that the stakes could not be higher and it is truly a matter of life and death—of heaven and hell.

I find it amazing that the Bible talks so little about hell and talks so much about Jesus, love, salvation, and eternal life. God's expectation appears to be that as soon as people hear the Good News they will be so drawn to God through his Son Jesus Christ, that they will believe the Good News and thereby have eternal life. Therefore, the bad news of hell is kind of irrelevant. That's why it comes down to such a personally important matter.

Believe, and you will delight the heart of God!

Part Five

THE PERFECT
FRIEND

CHAPTER TWENTY-SIX

THE SERVANT LORD

Almost everyone feels stressed and pressured at some time. We work long hours, and we struggle with the expectations others have of us and that we have of ourselves. It's true that we have lots of benefits—everything from cellular phones to multiple cars—but a growing number of Americans are beginning to wonder if it is really worth it.

Magazines regularly feature stories of successful professionals who sell their expensive homes, turn in the company car, quit high-paying jobs, and move to small towns with the goal of having a simpler life without the prestige, possessions, and pressures. Have you ever thought about doing that? Walking away from the rat race and getting a fresh start on a simpler level?

The Son of God stepped farther down than anyone ever has. Take a look at how the Bible describes what God's Son decided to do:

> Your attitude should be the same as that of Christ Jesus: Who, being in very nature God, did not consider equality with God something to be grasped, but made himself nothing, taking the

very nature of a servant, being made in human likeness. And being found in appearance as a man, he humbled himself and became obedient to death—even death on a cross! (Philippians 2:5–9)

Stepping Down

Jesus Christ did not hold tightly to position. This is absolutely amazing! Understand what the Son of God gave up. The Son had everything the Father has. He was the king of heaven. He got whatever he wanted. He lived in indescribable luxury. He was surrounded by magnificent beauty. He had unlimited wealth, power, and wisdom. Every angel of heaven was available for his service. He was at the top of the top—everyone and everything was below him.

To make some comparisons, he was a billion times richer than Bill Gates, more talented and creative than a country full of Michelangelos, more brilliant than a thousand Einsteins. He was more powerful than all of the monarchs, presidents, and dictators of history combined. He had it made! He was God!

Jesus Christ did not hold tightly to any of this. He was not possessive or greedy. He held everything with a loose grip, an open palm. Not that he didn't value all he had, but he was willing to let go of everything.

That is a sharp contrast to some people of high position and great power. For many of us, when we have position and power, we stretch to get more. We like to defend our territory. Whenever we can wedge in a word, we like to brag about our house, our car, the office where we work, our salary, or our net worth. Frankly, many of us hold so tightly to what we have that our knuckles are white and our lives are stressed with possessiveness and fear.

As if all of that were not amazing enough, when Jesus came to earth, he was willing to serve. I think it would have been more understandable if the Son of God had come to earth in order to rule. It might have made more sense if he came like an entrepreneur to build a large business empire in some distant place and to tell people what to do. But not Jesus. He came not to be served but to serve. It's as though he came with job application in hand, and in the space asking, "Position desired," he wrote only one word: *servant.*

Jesus was not only willing to serve, but he did serve. He worked hard as a craftsman in a carpenter's shop. He got down and dirty with people who were poor and sick, touching those with communicable diseases. He got down on his hands and knees and washed the feet of his followers. The aristocrats of his day were uncomfortable with his simplicity and his servanthood, but the vast majority of ordinary people were thrilled that he became one of them.

Imagine that Jesus is bodily here now and we have the opportunity to talk to him. When we ask him his name, he answers simply, "Jesus." Detecting a slight accent in the way he speaks, we sense that he has come from somewhere else. Ask him where he used to live, and he answers, "Heaven." If we ask about his

Ordinary people were thrilled that Jesus became one of them.

previous job, he would have to say, "I ran the universe." ("Who, being in very nature God, did not consider equality with God something to be grasped, but made himself nothing, taking the very nature of a servant, being made in human likeness.")

And that's not all. Jesus humbled himself to obey. It is one thing to *proudly* be a servant, to have a straight back and a certain stare, so that even in a servant role one retains some type of personal power. It is quite another thing to humbly be a servant who submits to the orders of others.

Suppose that one day you are driving across the company parking lot. There's ice and snow on the lot, but around the edges of the pavement it's turned to mud. Not paying attention, you overturn a corner and slide off the pavement so that your car gets stuck in the mud. The harder you try to get it out, the deeper the wheels sink.

While you're trying to figure out what to do next, you see in your rearview mirror a man in a suit and realize it is the president of the company. He volunteers to push. You are stunned and say, "Thanks for offering, but I don't think it would be a good idea. You would get filthy. I'll get somebody else to help." But he insists. He stands ankle deep in the mud pushing. As your car pulls out, the mud spins up and covers him from head to foot. As you roll down your window to thank him you think to yourself, "Wow! There is a truly great and humble man." Actually, you're probably thinking, "That would never happen at my company!"

Compare that to a completely different scene, where the company president takes a leave of absence. He gets a job on the night shift cleaning the parking lot where you park your car. As you are leaving, you slide on the ice and your car gets stuck in the mud. You see the man working, roll down your window, and call out, "Hey, I'm late for an appointment; come push my car." When he's back there, you rev the engine, splattering mud all over him, but the wheels catch and you go rocketing out without stopping to thank him because you're late. That's more like the experience of Jesus, the Son of God: "Being found in appearance as a man, he humbled himself and became obedient."

Jesus even obeyed the order to die. You know he didn't have to. They never could have crucified him if he had not consented. He could have called it off. He could have called legions of angels to control every circumstance, but he didn't. He decided to obey the most unjust order that was ever given to any servant in all of history.

He decided to do it because of his love for us. God's Son knew it was the only way he would ever reach us. He knew he could never reach us with words alone, for we would probably misunderstand them or not listen to them. He knew that if he only gave laws, instead of complying, we would disobey; if he threatened punishment, we would rebel. He knew that the only way he could reach us was through love. And the only way that love would ever be believed is if he became one of us.

MAKING DECISIONS AS CHRISTIANS

It was a great decision when the Son of God decided to become human. What can we learn from Jesus for *our* great decisions? True, our greatest decisions are not near the magnitude of the Son's decision to become human. But our decisions about life and death, family, job, relationships, and possessions are still very important to us.

How, then, can we make our decisions? Read Philippians 2:5 again: "Your attitude should be the same as that of Christ Jesus." This is how Christians are to think when making decisions. Like Jesus, we should have an attitude of trust.

When Jesus left heaven, he left his powers and possessions in the hands of God the Father. When he was on earth, he had no independent use of his divine attributes. He used to know everything; he was omniscient. But when he came to earth, he became ignorant, knowing only the things that God the Father allowed him to know. He used to be all-powerful; he was omnipotent. He became weak, able to do only the things that God the Father gave him the power to do. He used to be everywhere; he was omnipresent. But he became limited, able to go only where the Father let him go.

Think of it as a blind trust, where he took everything he had and left it in the hands of God to do whatever God chose for him to do, having no control over it himself. That is the attitude Christians should have when making decisions. We put everything we have in a blind trust, with God in charge, and we fully trust him. We trust him to make the decision whether we live or die. We give him control over our money—to do whatever he chooses with it. We are convinced that if we have a great deal, it is not because of our great skill and ability, but because of his generosity. If we have little, we accept it as sufficient, trusting him fully even if our cup has only a drop in it. We trust him with our jobs, our children, our marriages, and every other relationship.

When we have that attitude of trust in the decisions we make, we do not need to hold so tightly. We can loosen our grip. We can relax as we truly trust God. We don't have to be so intense about defending our reputation. We don't have to be so defensive or so possessive. We don't have to hoard all the good stuff to ourselves. We don't have to envy other people because they have something that we don't have. Like Jesus, if we trust, we do not need to grasp.

Trust is not always easy. I doubt that it was easy for Jesus. We prefer to be in control and to have power. The truth is, God is trustworthy and does far better with everything that is ours than we could ever do.

Like Jesus, we should also have an attitude of service. Not because we have to, but because we want to. Remember, we're talking about an attitude. It is possible to hold the highest position in society and have an attitude of service, and it is possible to hold the lowest position in society and not have a servant's heart.

Ask yourself, "How could I serve others like Jesus did?" Do it without their ever knowing that you did it. Without any special recognition or promise of reward—just to be like Jesus. An attitude of service is a revolutionary power. It's revolutionary, because most people prefer to be served rather than to serve someone else. It's not natural to adopt this attitude of service. It's supernatural. It's like Jesus. And like Jesus, in addition to an attitude of trust and an attitude of service, we should have an attitude of humility.

An attitude of service is a revolutionary power.

I look at Jesus' life and I listen to him. And I am awed by the humility and obedience of this man. He didn't need anyone to know how important he was or how right he was. He graciously and kindly obeyed the orders of people far inferior to him. He never insisted on his own superiority, although he had every right. If Jesus could be like that when he is so much better than I, then I must adopt his attitude and do the same.

Recently I talked with a man whose name and position is familiar to many. He held one of the highest and most powerful business positions in the United States, until two years ago when he and his wife moved overseas. They lived for two years in a five-hundred-square-foot apartment and gave themselves simply and humbly to the Christian service of others.

I can't help but wonder if those to whom this couple went ever had any idea who he was. I wonder if they could begin to imagine what this couple left behind. I wonder if they had any idea what they could have been doing and where they could have been doing it. I think this couple would not have wanted them to know.

We are Christians. We are followers of Jesus Christ, who "being found in appearance as a man, humbled himself and became obedient to death—even death on a cross."

Would you like to take a revolutionary supernatural approach to the great decisions of your life? This approach promises to be fabulous, but not necessarily easy: "Your attitude should be the same as that of Christ Jesus." It is an attitude of trust, an attitude of service, and an attitude of humility.

CHAPTER TWENTY-SEVEN

IN THE PRESENCE OF GLORY

One of the most amazing events in the Bible gives us a fleeting glimpse behind the scenes in the running of the universe—from the movement of planets down to the finest details of every one of our personal lives. It is something about which few of us know. Only a little bit is revealed as the curtain is parted an inch or so. For a few seconds, the brilliant, blinding light of the glory of God shines through. The event is called the Transfiguration. Its sights and sounds are recorded in Matthew 17.

Let me warn you: Adjust your eyes to see what is here, because it's like looking directly at the sun. It's almost too bright to see.

> After six days Jesus took with him Peter, James and John the brother of James, and led them up a high mountain by themselves. There he was transfigured before them. His face shone like the sun, and his clothes became as white as the light. Just then there appeared before them Moses and Elijah, talking with Jesus.
>
> Peter said to Jesus, "Lord, it is good for us to be here. If you wish, I will put up three shelters—one for you, one for Moses and one for Elijah."

While he was still speaking, a bright cloud enveloped them, and a voice from the cloud said, "This is my Son, whom I love; with him I am well pleased. Listen to him!"

When the disciples heard this, they fell facedown to the ground, terrified. But Jesus came and touched them. "Get up," he said. "Don't be afraid." When they looked up, they saw no one except Jesus.

As they were coming down the mountain, Jesus instructed them, "Don't tell anyone what you have seen, until the Son of Man has been raised from the dead."

The disciples asked him, "Why then do the teachers of the law say that Elijah must come first?"

Jesus replied, "To be sure, Elijah comes and will restore all things. But I tell you, Elijah has already come, and they did not recognize him, but have done to him everything they wished. In the same way the Son of Man is going to suffer at their hands." Then the disciples understood that he was talking to them about John the Baptist. (Matthew 17:1–13)

A GLIMPSE OF GLORY

Let's climb that mountain along with Peter, James, John, and Jesus. Let's see if we can see what they saw. Let's see if we can catch a glimpse of the supernatural glory that is behind and beyond the material world that we are far more used to dealing with. Let's walk through the sequence of this astounding story.

First, is the background to the spectacular sights they saw. The first words seem rather routine, but very important: "After six days Jesus . . . led them up a high mountain." Why is the timeline so important? It's because of what took place previously, in Matthew 16. Understand that the people of that day, including the disciples of Jesus, were waiting for a Messiah who had been promised centuries before, and their hope was probably at an all-time high. Excitement ran everywhere. They were expecting a capable king, a political power, a spiritual Christ, and they all hoped it might be Jesus.

Do you recall how Peter answered Jesus' question "Who do you say I am"? He just blurted it out: "Jesus, you are the Christ, you are the son of the living God," and everyone gasped and waited to see what Jesus would say. And he said, "You're right. I am the Christ," and they were ecstatic. The euphoria reigned; everything they had hoped for and dreamed about was true. They were more excited than campaign workers at party headquarters on election night when their candidate wins. All of history had come together right there, at that moment, in their presence.

But then Jesus added something that just about blew them away. In Matthew 16:21, we are told, "From that time on Jesus began to explain to his disciples that he must go to Jerusalem and suffer many things . . . that he must be killed and on the third day be raised to life."

Peter was so offended that Jesus would even suggest the Messiah had to suffer or die that he took Jesus aside to straighten him out. Matthew says, "Peter took him aside and began to rebuke him. 'Never, Lord!' he said. 'This shall never happen to you!' " Jesus shot back to Peter, "Get behind me, Satan! You are a stumbling block to me; you do not have in mind the things of God, but the things of men." And then Jesus laid some very heavy news on his disciples. He said, "If anyone would come after me, he must deny himself and take up his cross and follow me" (Matthew 16:22–24).

Those disciples were in shock for six days. They expected to be winners. They expected everything to go well, that they would be triumphant. But Jesus said it was going to be tough and that they were going to suffer; and they couldn't believe it. A lot of people still don't believe it. Many are convinced that Christians should have easy lives, and when they read the words of Jesus, that suffering is an integral part of the Christian life, they go into complete denial. They skip those parts. They say, "No, it just can't be true. What Jesus is supposed to do is chase all of life's problems away. It's too much of a shock, because I don't want to suffer, I don't want it to be hard."

Six days later Jesus took them up a mountain, probably Mount Hermon, to the highest point. He did it in order to give to them hope that on the other side of the suffering was a glory that they never dreamed of. There, on the top of that mountain, before their eyes, they saw Jesus transfigured. The Greek word is *metamorphosis*, which means "change." It's the word we learned in biology class to describe the change of a caterpillar into a butterfly.

> *He gave them hope that on the other side of the suffering was glory.*

If you had never seen a caterpillar and you discovered one crawling up your leg one day, in your wildest imagination you would never guess that thing would ever become a butterfly. And if butterflies were flying by as you were trying to figure it out—you'd probably never make the connection. Even when you know it's true, it is still such a change of form that it is difficult to grasp.

Before their eyes, Jesus was transfigured—a metamorphosis. His face turned bright and brilliant, like the sun. His normally colored clothes turned white as light. It was like heaven on earth. It was the glory of Jesus, the Son of God, showing him as he really is, not as he had been since his birth in Bethlehem. Then two other men appeared with him, seemingly from nowhere: Moses, the first lawgiver, and Elijah, the first prophet.

You read this and think to yourself, "This sounds just too weird." Understand: this is not weird; this is reality. This is the reality of heaven, the reality of God, the reality of the way the universe really works. It's the reality of eternity. It is the reality of the "behind the scenes." Jesus let them see it so they wouldn't be so discouraged, so they wouldn't think that suffering was all there was. He wanted them to know that behind all that we experience is a brilliant, magnificent, genius God, brighter than ten thousand suns, more intelligent than a million geniuses, more powerful than every atomic weapon. This is the God who is in charge of all of life, which we only darkly and inadequately see. This is the reality that controls the circumstances of our world and of our lives. It was a spectacular sight.

Now Peter had to say something. Peter had a mouth problem. He should have kept quiet, because what he had to say was somewhat silly. Here was the glory of God revealed; it was magnificent. And Peter said, "Lord, it's certainly nice to be here. Why don't I put up three tents: one for Elijah—we could put that over here; one for Moses—we could put some tablets in it in case he wants to write another commandment or two; and we'll have one for you—over here." Nothing more was said about Peter's remark, because he was interrupted by God. Rather than let Peter babble on, God the Father enveloped them in a cloud of light that was even more spectacular than what they had already seen.

God himself spoke out loud. He said, "This is my Son, whom I love; with him I am well pleased. Listen to him!" In two sentences God said so much. He declared that Jesus was no ordinary man, that he was the Son of God, that he was God himself.

The disciples could handle the sights, but the voice of God knocked them flat. They fell facedown to the ground. The voice of God is a terrifying thing, and the brilliance of the presence of God is overwhelming, because God is awesome. God is bigger and greater and more magnificent and powerful than anything we could ever imagine. To hear him, and to sense his presence, is beyond anything of human comparison; it drops all mortals to the ground before him, just because of who he is. The presence and the words of God can terrify the calmest and most confident persons on earth.

But wait a minute. Is this the same God that we call Friend? Were they terrified of the same God who allows people on the street to routinely profane his name, to deny his existence, and to defy his laws? Yes, it is the same God before whom we shall all stand. We will all someday experience what Peter, James, and John experienced that day. I expect our response will be exactly the same. When we recognize that we are in the presence of God, and when he speaks a single syllable, we, too, will fall facedown before him, overwhelmed, shaken, and terrified by this awesome God.

Only Jesus is as human as we are human, yet as divine as God is divine. Jesus tenderly touched them and warmly spoke to them, telling them not to be afraid. There's a powerful line that comes later in the New Testament, in 1 Timothy 2:5. It says that there is one mediator between God and man, and that is the man, Christ Jesus. He is the only one who can bridge the gap between God and us. He is the only one who can stop us from being blown away by who and what God is. He is the only one who can make it possible for us to genuinely and rightly refer to God as our friend.

Jesus is the only one who can make it possible for us to genuinely and rightly refer to God as our friend.

They did what Jesus said. They got up. They went down the mountain, but did not speak, because they didn't know what to say. It was too fresh in their minds—the brilliance and the glory of God was burned into the screen of their memories. They would be able to see it forever. The sound of the voice of God still echoed in their ears. They would know that sound better than any sound they ever heard before or would ever hear again. They had seen the other side of reality, that which makes the universe work. Life was more than jobs, family, houses, pain, and pleasure. The mundane, everyday realities of life that fill our minds would never be the same for them again. Now they understood that behind it all was this great, magnificent, brilliant, articulate, awesome God.

It was Jesus who first spoke. He said to them, "Don't tell anyone what you've seen, until the Son of Man has been raised from the dead."

At first they must have thought to themselves, "Don't worry, we're not going to tell anybody, because we don't have any idea what to say. We don't have any vocabulary for something like this. We don't have any basis of comparison. We wouldn't know what to tell them." But on second thought, they must have said to themselves, "How can we keep quiet? How could anyone who has experienced God ever be silent? We need to tell the first person we see; we need to run to our families and to our friends—anyone and everyone needs to know; we have experienced God!" But Jesus told them to keep silent. He did that because he didn't want to be a spectacle. Jesus had set himself on a course to the cross. He had come to suffer and die, to pay the price for human sin, and he wanted nothing to distract him from his central mission in life. And so he told them to be quiet until after the Resurrection, and then they could tell it all.

When they finally did speak, it was to ask a really picky question—not totally inappropriate, not wrong, but trivial. The disciples asked Jesus, "What about the lawyers' teaching that Elijah has to come before the Messiah?" It was a technical, theological question, but I think there was more behind it than that. They were trying to figure it all out. They were trying to make sense out of life, which is what most of us do most of the time.

Jesus was so gracious. He didn't say that they were out of line; he answered them. He acknowledged the question and gave them an answer. He said, "John the Baptist filled that role. He was the prophet like Elijah in the Old Testament prophecies." But then Jesus redirected the conversation and used the "s" word, *suffering*. He reminded them that suffering is part of what it's all about. He wouldn't let them forget that John had suffered, that he would suffer, and that those who were his disciples would suffer as well. It was more than a reminder. It was telling them one more time that suffering is part of what it means to be a Christian, but the other side of suffering is the glory of God himself.

LESSONS FROM THE MOUNTAINTOP

What do we learn from this true story of the supernatural? Let me give you five quick lessons, and then you decide how to apply them.

Lesson 1 is that there is supernatural glory and power behind the scenes. Never be so ignorant, so narrow, so blinded to the truth as to think that what you see is what you get. Because there is a whole lot more to reality than anything that we see. The other side of reality, beyond what our physical senses see, is God himself, and that awesome God is in control.

Lesson 2 is that God is overwhelming, and we must never underestimate how great he is; but Jesus is always there to help us. Jesus, who is both human and divine, is the mediator between God and us. He is always, even to this day, ready with his tender touch and his warm words.

Lesson 3 is that suffering goes with glory. Never be surprised by suffering in this life, but never give up expecting the glory that God promises will come.

Lesson 4 is that Jesus has the answers to our trickiest and most technical questions. He is not put off by them and he is not offended. He is willing to have us ask and willing to answer any question we have, and he will not get hung up on some technical trivia.

> *Never give up expecting the glory that God promises will come.*

Lesson 5 is that mountaintop experiences, whether on the Mountain of Transfiguration or some other mountain in our own experience, are wonderful indeed. They are those moments in life, brief and few, when in an indescribable way we also experience God. But understand that normally no one lives on top of a mountain. Life is lived on the plains and in the valleys, in the ordinary circumstances of life. It is the memory of the mountain that gets us through until our eternal heavenly home. The same Jesus who is with us in our suffering is the Jesus who was transfigured on the mountain to show us the other side—the victory and the glory of God through Jesus Christ our Lord.

CHAPTER TWENTY-EIGHT

THE GIFT OF PEACE

One afternoon I received a telephone call from a lifelong friend who now lives in Tennessee. He and I went through school together, traveled Europe together as collegians, and have kept in contact off and on through the years, although it had been some time since we last talked.

I asked him how things were going, because he left a significant executive position with a national company in order to venture out and start his own business. I asked him if the company was yet profitable. He said that it had been a tough four years, and shared some of the business struggles, family stresses, and changes in his church. Then he said, "Leith, it's like the parable of Jesus where the farmer sows the seed and some of that seed starts to grow and is choked out by thorns. Jesus said that the thorns are the cares of this world." Then he said, "I've learned about what it means to be choked by the cares of this world."

Well, my friend is not alone. Whether in the hills of Tennessee or the plains of Minnesota, the cares of this world seem to flourish and to choke lots of lives. I'm not so naïve as to say that we are the only generation that has had such difficulties, because you don't have to do much reading or research to discover that is simply not the case. But it does seem to me that we live in a particularly problem-prone generation. Change is rapid and significant. Fifty years ago who would have guessed that a then unknown disease called AIDS would be rampant today? Or that the law enforcement officials would say that the tidal wave of illicit drugs in our country has reached a point where they are simply unable to stop it? Or that there would be so many fractured families and divorces today?

The result is a generation of people in desperate need of help. If ever people needed inner peace, surely it has to be now. We need a good word. A "good word" in Latin is called a *benediction*. And that's what we've got at the end of the second letter to the Thessalonians. Paul writes: "Now may the Lord of peace himself give you peace at all times and in every way. The Lord be with all of you" (2 Thessalonians 3:16).

There are actually two good words in this benediction: *peace* and *presence*.

PEACE

Peace is inner confidence from God. The dictionary definitions of peace are not the same as the peace of God. Dictionaries define peace as the absence of conflict, the absence of strife, or the absence of war. There is nothing positive about it, simply the absence of something else.

There are two large problems with defining peace as the absence of war. One is that 90 percent of history—and some would say most of life—is war. But there must be more to peace than just the absence of war. A good marriage has to be more than not fighting. Relationships at work have to be better than merely not arguing with the boss. God wants far more and far better than "no strife."

So God offers us divine peace. Divine peace is a deep inner confidence in God. In fact, it is possible to have the peace of God even in the midst of war. Divine peace is not dependent on outside circumstances. It can flourish even when external circumstances are absolutely the worst they can be.

Jesus demonstrated divine peace before he died. The authorities turned against him, his own disciples abandoned him, and he was tortured by pain when the soldiers crucified him. I think it is impossible for us to imagine any worse circumstances than those experienced by Jesus, and yet he demonstrated an internal peace that came from God.

Paul and Silas were first-century missionaries who came to the Greek city of Philippi, where they were arrested, illegally beaten, and thrown into a dungeon. Circumstances couldn't have been worse, but they sang hymns and praised God, giving encouragement to their fellow prisoners. They demonstrated this amazing peace of God.

It's not easy to describe. The peace of God is a focused conviction that God is in charge and that God is good. It is in knowing that he is sovereign, and that our relationship with God is a million times more important than anything else.

Sometimes it seems that we best understand God's inner peace against the backdrop of adversity—those times when things are not as we would choose. Some go through a time of extended unemployment. Others face chronic disease, mental illness, or a strained relationship. There are the unfulfilled dreams of the infertile couple, yearning for a baby; of the entrepreneur who stepped out in enormous faith with every bit of appropriate planning to begin a new company, but sees that it's failing.

The conviction that God loves us and that he will work all things for good carries us through.

Many things happen in life that we would not choose, but deep inside there comes a confidence that, in spite of all these things, God is there. He makes an amazing difference. The conviction that he loves us and that he will work all things for good carries us through. He promises that he will walk with us on the highest mountaintops, trudge with us through the worst of swamps. He will take us through the worst of all—the valley of death. That confidence is called the peace of God.

Some years ago there was a massive earthquake in Soviet Armenia. Large apartment buildings crumbled like sand castles, resulting in enormous loss of property and great loss of life. Rescue workers came from around the world to help. When everything finally settled down and the bodies were buried, an analysis was done. They concluded that the reason the tragedy was so great had to do with the construction of the buildings. The earthquake probably could not have been predicted, and surely it could not have been prevented. However, the construction of the buildings was without reinforcing steel; it was simply concrete. It looked fine and worked fine when the earth was stable. But when the tremors came, those buildings made only of concrete could not endure the trauma and they began to crumble. There were no steel rods running through the concrete to hold it together when the earth shook.

The peace of God is the steel reinforcement of the Christian's life. You can walk into a group of people and probably not tell the difference in external appearance between a Christian and a non-Christian. The "concrete" on the outside doesn't look a whole lot different. But the difference comes when the earth shakes and the tremors are frightening. Then, and sometimes only then, we discover whether or not we have the peace of God that is the reinforcing steel that holds us together in the earthquakes of life.

The peace of God is not something we simply conjure up and decide that we're going to have. We cannot suddenly decide, "I want to have those rods of reinforcement running through me so that when the tough times come I will be able to stand solid and firm." Frankly, it's not our choice to make. The benediction of 2 Thessalonians 3:16 explicitly says that this is a gift from God. "Now may the Lord of peace himself give you peace at all times and in every way."

It is God who gives us confidence in himself. It is God who gives us confidence in objective ways all the time, through the Bible, and through our life experiences and those of people around us. We have a continual flow of evidence that God is trustworthy.

But he also gives us a mystical shot of peace to fit our current need. When we are told that he gives peace *at all times* it refers to the different occasions. I take that not to mean all the time, but rather that in any circumstances of life when we desperately need reinforcement, he provides it appropriately at that occasion. And he provides it *in every way*. The particular Greek word that Paul uses here means "at every turning."

The road of life includes all kinds of different terrains and turns. What God gives to us is a peace that is for "all times and for every turning." It is a peace that enables us to soar to the highest heaven and not be proud. And it is a peace that enables us to walk through the deepest hell of circumstances and not fall into despair.

PRESENCE

Peace is the first good word in this benediction. The second good word is *presence.* "The Lord be with you all." When Jesus promised that he would be with Christians, he was not simply using a figure of speech. He was not merely giving us verbal comfort. He truly meant it.

Jesus is with us as "real-ly" as we are with each other. He is omnipresent—able to be all places at the same time. This had to be hard for first-century Christians to understand and believe. In that time it was generally thought the only things that were real were those things that could be experienced by one or more of our five senses. We know better. We know, for example, that it is possible for radon gas to come up through our basement and expose us to danger, in spite of the fact that it cannot be seen, smelled, tasted, heard, or felt. Even though you can't see it, it's real. We know what gravity is and does, but we can't see it except in terms of the effect that it has.

We know reality is not necessarily tied to the experience of our five senses. With our understanding of modern science it is probably easier for us to understand the reality of the invisible God being with us and giving us peace even when we cannot touch him, see him, or hear him.

But there is an inadequacy to the analogy to radon gas or gravity, because they are natural phenomena and Jesus Christ is supernatural. He is not limited in what he can do. He is God! And because he is supernatural he can give supernatural peace. He can give peace inside when we are scared outside. He can be the steel reinforcement in our lives when all the earth is shaking around us. He can do in us and for us what naturally cannot be done. He is supernatural and he is present.

Because Jesus Christ is supernatural he can give supernatural peace.

I grew up not far from the Atlantic Ocean, and to this day I dearly love the sea. As a boy I often went to the beach. I learned the joys and dangers of the ocean at a young age. It's fun to float in the Atlantic. The waves come one after the other, and you can jump into them and have the froth of the sea all over you. It's an exciting experience, but dangerous undercurrents also can carry you out to sea. You can be playing in the waves when an unexpectedly large wave comes and bashes against you, taking your breath away. Like life, the ocean is fun and frightening at the same time.

One of my favorite boyhood memories is swimming in the ocean with my father. It was a completely different experience than swimming alone. Somehow the fear wasn't there. When he came with me we could go out far over my head. We could ride the waves and still be safe. I didn't think at all about the undercurrents. That which otherwise might be fearful was changed to laughter. I can even now remember the feel of his strong body with my arms tightly wrapped around his neck. His presence did not eliminate the dangers, but his presence gave me peace!

"Now may the Lord of peace himself give you peace at all times and in every way. The Lord be with all of you." Amen.

CHAPTER TWENTY-NINE

THE CURING TOUCH

Leprosy is a terrible disease. It causes a thickening of the skin in the hands, feet, and other parts of the body. It causes skin lesions and does a lot of nerve damage. Often the hands and feet curl up, claw-like, so they cannot be used. Because the hands, feet, and limbs lose feeling, they are prone to serious accidents. The body is often disfigured after years of leprosy—sometimes terribly and hideously so. It is a disease that progresses slowly and tragically.

The disease isn't called leprosy anymore; it's called Hansen's disease, named after a physician in Norway who in 1874 discovered the bacteria that causes the disease. Today there are drugs for the treatment of Hansen's disease, and people are no longer isolated but are typically treated as outpatients. It's estimated that the number of people who suffer from leprosy, or Hansen's disease, in the United States today is somewhere short of seven thousand.

If you read through the Bible, you'll find many mentions of leprosy. Actually, the leprosy of the Bible was not always Hansen's disease but any one of a number of skin ailments, all collectively referred to as leprosy. Whatever the name or specific ailment, leprosy was greatly feared and those infected with it were often isolated.

Let me take you to the day that Jesus preached the Sermon on the Mount—the most famous and scintillating sermon ever preached. Matthew 8:1–4 tells us what happened afterward.

> When [Jesus] came down from the mountainside, large crowds followed him. A man with leprosy came and knelt before him and said, "Lord, if you are willing, you can make me clean."
>
> Jesus reached out his hand and touched the man. "I am willing," he said. "Be clean!" Immediately he was cured of his leprosy. Then Jesus said to him, "See that you don't tell anyone. But go, show yourself to the priest and offer the gift Moses commanded, as a testimony to them."

THE MAN WITH LEPROSY

As I read this story I find it sad that the man's name is not mentioned. He was known merely by his disease. In most cases that was all people wanted to know about a person with leprosy. But I suppose we do pretty much the same thing today. We tend to label people by their problems or their peculiarities or their professions. We might forget a name, but say, "Oh, I know who you're talking about; he's the alcoholic, and she's the divorcee." Actually we categorize people by some ugly names because of their situations.

In the first century, lepers received very particular treatment in Palestine. The law required that once a person was diagnosed with leprosy, he or she could no longer have any association with healthy persons. People with leprosy had to wear torn clothing and disheveled, unkempt hair whenever they went out in public, and were required to put their hands over their upper lip, shouting out for everyone to hear, "Unclean! Unclean!" They always had to identify themselves as lepers. On a calm day the law required that no one could come within six feet of anyone who had leprosy. On a windy day no one could come closer than 150 feet.

Josephus, a Jewish historian of the first century, says that persons with leprosy were treated as if they were, in effect, dead men. Ancient literature has some particularly interesting and painful things to say about the relationship between rabbis and persons with leprosy. One is the account of a rabbi who refused to eat an egg that had been purchased at a market on a street where a leper once had walked. Another rabbi boasted that he always carried stones to throw to make sure that lepers would keep a suitable and legal safe distance. Do you get the picture? Lepers were despised. They were avoided. They were ostracized. They were considered disgusting.

Knowing all that, can you imagine the response of first-century Jews who witnessed a rabbi named Jesus reach out his hand and touch a leper? They must have been stunned.

Consider the options of this man. The record simply says that a man with leprosy came. For him to come into a crowd, aside from breaking the law and hearing the insults, he risked his life that they would pick up stones and kill him. I'm impressed by this unnamed man with this terrible disease. Impressed that he was proactive rather than reactive. Impressed that he chose to believe rather than to blame. I'm impressed that instead of complaining about his malady, he came to Jesus for help.

Instead of complaining about his malady, he came to Jesus for help.

Throughout the centuries people have always faced great difficulties. They would point an accusing finger at us today because we spend so much of our energy and resources blaming others for our problems. As a generation we blame our parents or blame our schools or government or church or spouse or children for our problems. Perhaps we should tear a page out of the biography of the unnamed man with leprosy. He did not blame others, although certainly he must have gotten the disease from somebody. He did not complain, although unquestionably his sickness was serious. Instead, he did something. He came to Jesus.

Actually, the Bible says that a man with leprosy came and knelt before Jesus, but the Greek word *knelt* is almost always translated elsewhere in the Bible and in other ancient literature as "worshiped." It was a risky thing to do, for to worship someone was to acknowledge that person to be God. He could be accused of blasphemy. And he would put Jesus at risk as well, for already there were those who severely criticized Jesus for allegations they thought he made concerning his own deity. But this man didn't seem to care. He saw that Jesus was worthy of worship, and so he just did it, pushing all the risks aside.

COME TO JESUS

When we find ourselves dealing with life's leprosies, we too should come to Jesus. Let us not be so consumed with our problems that we fail to first see who he is and to worship him as the Son of God and Lord of all. We need to do what the leper did, understanding that worship always precedes asking.

The man with leprosy spoke, "Lord, if you are willing, you can make me clean." He had absolute faith in the ability of Jesus to cure him—to do what no priest or physician could do. His words did not demand healing. He simply declared his faith that Jesus could do it if he chose to do it.

I have often wondered how I would respond if I had a diagnosis of some terrible disease. I've seen a lot of people in my life and a lot of different maladies, and I've learned that there is a great deal of difference between knowing someone with cancer and having cancer yourself. Knowing someone who has AIDS is certainly not the same thing as having AIDS. There are miles of difference between visiting someone who has a debilitating disease and being that person.

There is probably no way of guessing how I might respond or react when my turn comes, but I can tell you, from today's perspective at least, I would like to be like this man who came to Jesus. I expect that I would want to be healed as much as he wanted to be healed. If need be, I would push my way through crowds regardless of what people might think. While I know I must be responsible to seek appropriate medical treatment, I would like to think that I would come to Jesus, believing with all of my heart that ultimately he can do that which no physician could ever do. I want to have absolute confidence and faith that he can heal me. But I would also like to think that I would trust Jesus enough to leave it to him. If he chooses, he can make me well.

If Jesus chooses, he can make me well.

Jesus reached out his hand and touched him. He touched the untouchable. He put himself at risk. He broke the rules. The crowd must have gasped. I suspect that there were people who had listened to Jesus on the mountaintop and were enthralled by him, who, when they saw him touch that man with leprosy, turned around and walked away because they were never going to follow a man who would do such a despicable thing. There were others, I imagine, who kicked the ground with their feet trying to find rocks they might throw to stone the leper or to stone the rabbi who touched him.

There is something very special about a touch. Especially when you're alone, or when you're scared, when you've got to deal with what you've got to deal with all by yourself. Well, Jesus wasn't afraid of the risks. It meant everything to that desperate man when Jesus touched him, because it meant that Jesus cared more about him than what the people thought. Jesus cared more about him than the rules, regulations, and laws that kept everyone else away. Jesus saw him and touched him as a man who really mattered.

Most of us will probably never see a case of leprosy—even those who have careers in medicine. Yet society is loaded with untouchables—just with different names. All the people that the crowd splits for, all the people who have labels instead of names, all the people who appear to be dangerous and uncomfortable. Some studies have shown that as a person with a terminal illness comes closer and closer to death, physicians, sometimes families, and friends come to visit far less often—in order to keep their distance from the dying.

There is a special comfort for you who have been abandoned by others, from whom society has kept a distance. Maybe it's because of cancer, or AIDS, because of the color of your skin, or the number of your years, or how much money you have, or how much money you don't have. It might be because of some crime you committed or sin of which you are guilty or maybe because of bankruptcy, addiction—whatever has labeled you. Hear the good news! While the crowds may keep their distance, while your friends may forsake you, while your family may be ashamed of you, and while even the church may treat you like a leper, Jesus will reach out and touch you. We do not embarrass him; he is not ashamed when we come to him. He is not turned off by the labels that have replaced our names. He cares. He accepts us as the persons that we are. He reaches out and touches us.

To his touch, Jesus added these tender words: "I'm willing." He was willing to use his power to meet that man's needs.

And when Jesus spoke again, he simply said, "Be clean!"

A MIRACLE CURE

Matthew says the man was immediately cured of his leprosy. How do you suppose such a thing works? If we were to analyze this from a scientific perspective, how would we explain it? Was it some sort of psychosomatic malady that affected his skin because of emotional distress? Was he so convinced that Jesus could cure him that when Jesus spoke there was a psychological conversion that affected his body so that it appeared he was cured? Or do you think he really didn't have the disease in the first place? Were all these folk who had been listening up on the mountain so mesmerized by Jesus that they believed something happened that in reality did not? What do you think really happened?

Let's not forget that we aren't talking about some ordinary man. We are speaking of the Son of God, the Lord of all. It was he who created the universe by speaking a word, so it's true that his word does things that our word does not do. I believe that a true miracle took place. Because it was a miracle, it's beyond our explanation.

However, it raises all kinds of questions for us today. Can such miracles happen now? Does the Christ still cure? The answer is a resounding "Yes!" That brings up another question: "Why don't I see the kind of miracles today that happened then?" Perhaps it's because we don't come as that leper came. Or because we do not worship as that leper worshiped. Or because we do not believe as that leper believed. Or because Jesus does not always choose to do something as he did that day.

We cannot control the choices of Jesus, but we can accept them as wise and good. We can come and worship, and we can believe.

So let me say it straight out—take your diseases and your difficulties to Jesus Christ. Worship him; believe him; tell him your needs; and tell him that you trust him to do what is right. When you do, you will be amazed to feel his touch and to see his miracles.

Take your diseases and your difficulties to Jesus Christ.

Jesus did not cure and run. He gave follow-up directions. He said, "See that you don't tell anyone. But go, show yourself to the priest and offer the gift that Moses commanded, as a testimony to them." It's surprising that Jesus told the man to be quiet because I'm sure he wanted to tell everyone he possibly could. But understand that

Jesus was on a far greater mission than curing someone of a terrible disease. He was on his way to the cross to cure all humankind of the far greater eternal disease, sin. He did not want his timetable to be interrupted by a sudden popularity that would arouse the suspicion of the Roman authorities.

Jesus asked the man to be quiet and follow the prescribed Hebrew law—to be examined by a priest, to offer sacrifices, and to go through a whole course of events so that it could be clearly documented that a miracle had taken place. Beyond that, Jesus wanted to connect the man to the spiritual community that could meet his continuing needs.

Imagine with me that we were to cast this story as a play. What would be your part? Would you be one of the crowd coming down from the mountain, watching everything that was happening? Or do you think that you might play the part of the leper? Are you an observer to others' needs, or are you someone who has a great need that Jesus can meet?

If you would choose to play the part of the one with leprosy, let me try your imagination one more time. Suppose we were to update the script and cast it in contemporary times, so that the difficulty would not be leprosy, but whatever your difficulty is. What would that be?

You see the picture. You get the point. Come to Jesus with whatever is the greatest need in your life. Kneel down before him and worship him. Tell him that you fully believe that he can do whatever needs to be done in your life and that you fully trust him to do what is best.

CHAPTER THIRTY

BORN TO WIN

The problems encountered by Olympic champions are what enable them to win the prize. If they didn't have stress, pressure, and problems to deal with, they would lose. One article stated: "For today's Olympians, as with those of the past, the ultimate proof of toughness lies not in the means but the end: standing on the highest platform when the medals are handed out."[1]

Does it surprise you to realize that this same news item was also written almost two thousand years ago in the New Testament? Picturing Christians as the athletes and using the ancient Olympics as a metaphor, James 1:12 says: "Blessed is the man who perseveres under trial, because when he has stood the test, he will receive the crown of life that God has promised to those who love him."

This verse ought to be written on a three-by-five card and taped to the dashboard of our car, stuck to the refrigerator, or committed to

---

[1] *U.S. News and World Report*, Feb. 14, 1994, 52.

memory. These words help us to understand the toughest times of our lives and to interpret them for good. Admittedly, it has sort of a surprising beginning.

STICKING IT OUT

"Blessed is the person who perseveres under trial." *Blessed* means "happy." It's saying that true happiness is found by persevering under difficulty or trial. It's not saying that troubles or problems or difficulties themselves make us happy, but that those who face them and persevere end up being happy as a result.

A good feeling comes from being a survivor. To face difficulty of any kind is like going into a fight with an enemy who is trying to get us down. When we hang in there and survive the fight we are the victors instead of the victims. The victors have a genuine happiness as a result. It can be a very good feeling! We feel good about God for helping us through. We feel good about ourselves for enduring. We feel strong and successful and thankful because we made it.

That's what James means when he tells us to "Be happy! Blessed are you when you stick it out under trials." But *persevere* means more than just survival. It means fighting back against evil with good. It's not passive. I think of it this way: Everybody has problems—that's obvious. You could call them "bad things."

How do we respond? Some of us respond by running away. We quit the job, leave the relationship, move out of town, or simply go and hide. That's not what the Bible has in mind.

There are other people who don't fight back, they simply give in. When the problems come they surrender to them. They let the bad guys take over their lives. That's definitely not what the Bible is talking about.

Some people fight back with good. If someone is unkind, they are kind. When someone else is unforgiving, they forgive. When they fail to get their own way, their Christian commitment grows and their Christian character shines in these worst of circumstances.

I was talking to a friend about an experience he had last year. He told me about a man who was diagnosed with cancer and died a relatively short time later. They had a number of conversations over the several months between diagnosis and death. Each time he saw this man he said it seemed as if his body had shrunk and his soul had grown.

Now, that's persevering under trial! That's showing that no disease is going to conquer him. Even if he died he would grow in godliness and character. It may look as if the cancer won and he lost, but the truth is, he won, because "blessed is the man who perseveres under trial."

It's finishing the race that really counts.

I often think about the importance of finishing well. Anyone can talk about success or victory. Anyone can start a race. Anyone can claim to be a Christian. But it's finishing the race that really counts. It's sticking with it through the hard times, it's getting back up when you stumble and going on, it's remaining faithful, it's persevering under the inevitable trials that are part of every life's experience.

When I complete all the things that God has called me to be and to do—and I die, I don't want God or anyone else to talk about how well I started. They can even skip what I've done along the way. For me, the best thing of all would be for others to say, "He finished well." I can't think of anything better to have written on a tombstone than "He finished well." If that can be said about me, then I'll be a happy man, because "blessed is the man who perseveres under trial."

The Crown to Come

A big part of that happiness for Christians is the reward we will receive. The second part of James 1:12 says, "Because when he has stood the test he will receive the crown of life." The word *crown* came straight out of the Olympic games. It's the Greek word *stephanos*, from which we get the name Stephen. The *stephanos*, or crown, was the wreath given to the winners of the Olympic events, much like the gold, silver, and bronze medals given today. It was the highest honor and was worn by the victors long after the ceremony was over as an expression of great pride.

James explains to Christians that we have "the crown of life" waiting for us at the end of life's race. It's better than a wreath, better than Olympic gold. It is the crown of eternal life that we get to wear forever. It is the symbol of faithfulness and of finishing well.

When it comes to rewards, a lot of us don't want to wait—we'd prefer the gold medal now. But that's not the way it works.

Olympic athletes don't get the gold for starting the race. They don't get silver or bronze medals simply for qualifying. In the process of preparation, if an athlete is injured, no medals are given. The medals are not given for encouragement halfway through the race. Medals are given for *finishing*. As long as they know that the prize is waiting at the end, the athletes keep practicing; they persevere.

It's the same for Christians. Do we get tired? Do we get stressed out? Do we get pressured? Do we stumble and trip and not want to get up again? Do we have those days when we say, "I just cannot go on"? Yes, of course. We all do. Those problems are our opportunities to live Christianly, to show what it's like for a Christian to deal with difficulties. It is not bad news but good news, as strange as it sounds, because "blessed is the man who perseveres under trial, because when he has stood the test, he will receive the crown of life."

The question is, can I do this? "I don't know if I can. I'm not sure that I'm able to keep going on. I don't think I can hold up and remain faithful under stress. I'm not sure I can persevere under trial or live Christianly when dealing with the big-time problems of life."

But God says, "Yes, you can!"

The answer is yes for those who love God and believe God's promises and call him Friend. "Blessed are you who persevere under trial, because when you have stood the test, you will receive the crown of life *that God has promised to those who love him.*"

We don't become Christians because we win; we win because we're Christians. When a person loves God and accepts Jesus Christ as Savior, that person becomes a Christian. Christians are born winners regardless of their past, because at that moment of rebirth, God does something in our spiritual genes that transforms every Christian into a winner. God promises that every person who is a Christian will persevere under trial and will receive the crown of life that God has waiting.

Christians are born winners regardless of their past.

I heard a story about a woman who was the cook and director of food service at a Christian camp in the western United States for over fifty years. During all those years she followed a common camp practice of providing only one fork per person per meal. When the dishes were collected after the main course, before the dessert, campers were always instructed to "hold on to your fork, because the best is yet to come." She said it so many thousands of times that she became known for that phrase.

Before she died she made a request both unusual and memorable. She specified that at her death she be laid in her casket and buried with a fork in her hand. Not only did the fork symbolize her life, but she also wanted to communicate her conviction that "the best is yet to come."

How did James say it? "Blessed is the one who perseveres under trial, because when you have stood the test, you will receive the crown of life that God has promised to those who love him."

Are you facing trials that are difficult and hard? With Jesus you will win. So hold on—because the best is yet to come!

CHAPTER THIRTY-ONE

LOVED BY GOD

I was at a retreat center in Colorado Springs with a group of about twenty-five men. One evening our discussion came around to the topic of fathers and the impact that our fathers had had on our lives. The general thrust of the discussion was appreciation. The men expressed gratitude for the amount of time their fathers had spent with them when they were young boys. But one man's words were especially memorable. I knew this man quite well and admired and respected him. He said that his father did not treat him well and was not a good influence. He felt the best thing his father ever did was not to spend much time with him. Sad to say, he was better off without his father's influence.

Certainly that is not true with our heavenly Father. He is the best influence we can have. And one of the best parts about God the Father is his love.

No one knows more about the love of the Father than Jesus. In a prayer recorded in John 17, Jesus prayed to the Father specifically for us.

"My prayer is not for them alone. I pray also for those who will believe in me through their message, that all of them may be one, Father, just as you are in me and I am in you. May they also be in us so that the world may believe that you have sent me. I have given them the glory that you gave me, that they may be one as we are one: I in them and you in me. May they be brought to complete unity to let the world know that you sent me and have loved them even as you have loved me.

"Father, I want those you have given me to be with me where I am, and to see my glory, the glory you have given me because you loved me before the creation of the world." (John 17:20–24)

Jesus prays for "those who will believe in me." He was praying for us specifically during his lifetime 2000 years ago, and he still is! He goes on to say that God the Father loves us as he loves Jesus: "You sent me and have loved them even as you have loved me." That is an amazing declaration. We can understand how God the Father can have great love for his Son, but it is a difficult stretch to understand how he can love us as he loves his Son.

At the end of these verses, Jesus says that God the Father loved him "before the creation of the world." That means that before the world came into being, before there was sin or Satan, before there was any-thing—God loved. God is a lover. Love is not primarily what God does. Love is primarily who God is.

GOD IS LOVE

"God is love" (1 John 4:16) is a profound and wonderful truth, but it is sometimes misjudged or misinterpreted. Some people try to twist it and reverse the order. They claim that if God is love, then love is God. To say that love is godlike is changing the meaning. We can say that blood is red, but we can't reverse that and say that everything that is red is blood. "God is love" means that love is essential to the essence and character of God. If you can imagine God without love you have imagined someone who is not God at all.

It is very important to understand that the love of God comes from who he is and not who we are. First John 4:10 is very direct: "This is love: not that we loved God, but that he loved us and sent his Son as an atoning sacrifice for our sins."

When God loves us it's not because we're likable. It's not because we're attractive. It's not because of what we say. It's not because of what we do. The love that God has for us begins not in reaction to us but in the fact that God is a lover. Love always comes from him because of who he is—not in response to who we are.

> *Love always comes from God because of who he is—not in response to who we are.*

You know how people say, "I saw her and it was love at first sight!" That is saying that I was really attracted to the way she looked. Or "I remember the first day that we met. He was just wonderful! He was so kind and he said all the right things. I laughed at his jokes, and our personalities were magnetically attracted, and I fell in love with him!" That's a common way for us to think. We love someone because of the way he or she is. But if that person changes, we can decide we don't love that person anymore. We talk about falling in love, but we also talk about falling out of love. If the person toward whom we were so drawn becomes unattractive, we can say, "Well, I used to love her [or I used to love him], but I don't anymore."

What this does is describe love on the basis of the other person's lovability rather than on the basis of our lovingness. It's just not that way with God. The love of God starts with who he is and is not dependent upon who we are or what we are like.

God looks at us even in our worst moments and says, "I love you." God loves boys and girls and men and women who others would say are not attractive and who do not deserve that kind of love. But it's good news that we don't have to be handsome or beautiful or intelligent. We do not have to be well-educated or perfect or personable. God loves us because of who he is. He intensely loves us. It is God-love.

God's love eternally gives to others. Paul wrote of his personal experience of God's love in Galatians 2:20: "The life I live in the body, I live by faith in the Son of God, who loved me and gave himself for me."

God's attitude of love is a desire to always do what is in the best interest of those whom he loves. That is a powerful and transforming realization. I think being loved changes the way people live. It changes the way we think of ourselves.

We see people who have been unloved for a long time and the deep and terrible toll it takes on their lives. Then when they are loved, sud denly self-worth soars. Confidence is increased. They become different persons. It is even more so with the love of God. When we begin to understand that God really loves us, we have a motivation for living. Then we see ourselves differently than we saw ourselves before. That is one of the huge differences between Christians and non-Christians. Non-Christians go through life wondering if they are loved. Relationships may come and go, and there's no continuity. But as Christians, we know we are greatly loved, and we are not dependent on human love that can change. If someone falls out of love with us, as painful as that may be, we know that we are still loved by God.

Jesus, in one of the great lines in the New Testament, said, "Greater love has no one than this, that he lay down his life for his friends" (John 15:13). Just saying it is not enough. God not only wants what is best for those he loves, he does what is best for those he loves.

The greatest example is that God the Father sent his Son to die for us. The Son of God agreed to come and to die on the cross. He did it for us because he loves us—because we are his friends. That is God-sized love! That is astonishing. That is overwhelming. It's love in action that Jesus gave his life out of love for us.

On those days when you're feeling unloved or maybe even forgotten, when it seems as if God does not answer your prayers, or certainly does not answer them the way you would choose for them to be answered, see the cross. Remember the words in John 3:16: "God so loved the world that he gave his one and only Son, that whoever believes in him shall not perish but have eternal life." Understand that the God who loved us enough to send his Son is certainly not going to let us down. He's not going to abandon us. Understand that God's love will always be his eternal attitude expressed in his sacrificial action.

LOVING GOD

How do we respond to God's love? In one of Jesus' most important teachings he told us what we're supposed to do: "Love the Lord your God with all your heart and with all your soul and with all your mind" (Matthew 22:37). That is to say, we are to love God the same way he loves us. We are to have an attitude of love toward God and do that which is best for God. We are to love God passionately and completely with heart and soul and mind.

So how do you get to loving God with heart and soul and mind? The place to begin is to focus on God and his love. Read about it; consume every piece of information available about the love of God; memorize it; meditate upon it; thank God for his love; worship God for his love. It is God's love for us that triggers our love for him. It's not as if we can somehow generate it ourselves. And when we are tempted to say or to do things that will hurt God, our best remedy is to return to his love for us. Be loved by God, and you will love him.

In Matthew 22:39, Jesus added something very important when he said, "Love your neighbor as yourself." The love of God is so wonderful and so filling that it changes us and then overflows to others. I'm convinced that when we experience the love of God we ourselves become different. We have a different attitude toward ourselves. We love ourselves—not in the sense of being narcissistic or selfish—but in the sense that we want the very best for ourselves in the same way that God wants the very best for us. We turn away from self-destructive behavior. We turn away from selfishness. We begin to have right attitudes and right actions toward ourselves as we fill up with this love of God. And then we are able to love others as God loves us.

Then we love from the love inside us. Then we love others independently of the way they are, independent of the way they look, independent of what they do. In other words, we are to love others as God loves us.

Then we love from the love inside us.

It's great in theory, but some people are exceptionally difficult to love. We fall into a common trap and blame the other person. We say that we can't love people because they are impossible to love. We become highly critical of others because we need a good excuse for not loving them. But that is to misunderstand the whole matter. God's way is that he loves us on the basis of who he is, not who we are. And we are to love others not on the basis of who they are, but on the basis of who we are as those who are loved by God. God is love. God loves us. We respond to that love by loving him and ourselves and others.

Moses Mendelssohn was the grandfather of the famous German composer. Moses Mendelssohn was not a handsome man, and he knew it. He was very short in stature, and he had a back deformity that in that day was called a "humpback." He took a business trip to visit a merchant in the German city of Hamburg. While he was there he met the beautiful daughter of the merchant. Frumtje was her name. He was enthralled by her, but she'd have nothing to do with him. She was repulsed by his appearance. After several days of attempting conversation with her, he got up his courage for one last attempt. He spoke to her.

But she didn't answer. She never even looked his way. In a last attempt, he asked her a question: "Do you believe marriages are made in heaven?"

She didn't look at him, but she answered him, "Yes. Do you believe marriages are made in heaven?"

Moses Mendelssohn answered, "Yes, I do. You see, in heaven, at the birth of each boy, the Lord announces which girl he will marry. When I was born, my future bride was pointed out to me. Then the Lord added, 'But your wife will be humpbacked.' Right then and there I called out, 'Oh, Lord, a humpbacked woman would be a tragedy. Please, Lord, give me the hump and let her be beautiful.' " According to the story, Frumtje looked into his eyes and then reached out her hand and touched him. Something deep inside of her had been stirred. She gave him her hand, and later became his lifelong wife.[1]

Now compare that to the far greater love that God has for us. Love that is indescribable. Love that will not give up. Love that will not let us go. Love that volunteered Jesus Christ his Son to take the agony and deformities of death on a cross before we were born. Even when God speaks and we refuse to turn our heads or listen to what he says or acknowledge that he's there, he still loves us.

God is great; God is good; God is holy; God is love; and God is knowable. When we begin to understand his love, our eyes and hearts turn to him, and we reach out our hands and tell him we love him and want to spend the rest of our lives and eternity with him. Then we can call him Savior, Lord, Father, and Friend.

---

[1]Barry and Joyce Vissell, "True Love," *The Wolfville Gazette*, vol. 3, issue 1, August 1997. Published by OMNI Electronics, Nova Scotia, Canada.